ALSO BY MARY BUFFETT AND DAVID CLARK

Buffettology

The Buffettology Workbook

The New Buffettology

THE TAO

of

WARREN BUFFETT

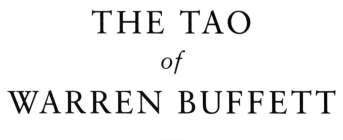

Warren Buffett's Words of Wisdom

Quotations and Interpretations to Help Guide You to
Billionaire Wealth and Enlightened Business Management

MARY BUFFETT *and* DAVID CLARK

Scribner

NEW YORK   LONDON   TORONTO   SYDNEY

SCRIBNER
1230 Avenue of the Americas
New York, NY 10020

SCRIBNER and design are trademarks of
Macmillan Library Reference USA, Inc., used under license
by Simon & Schuster, the publisher of this work.

For information about special discounts for bulk purchases,
please contact Simon & Schuster Special Sales:
1-800-456-6798 or business@simonandschuster.com

Designed by Kyoko Watanabe
Text set in Classical Garamond

Manufactured in the United States of America

3   5   7   9   10   8   6   4   2

Library of Congress Cataloging-in-Publication Data is available.

ISBN-13: 978-1-4165-4132-5
ISBN-10: 1-4165-4132-2

For
our good friend and fellow Buffettologist
Bob Eisenberg

CONTENTS

THE TAO
of
WARREN BUFFETT

INTRODUCTION

For twelve years, from 1981 to 1993, I was the daughter-in-law of Warren Buffett, the world's most successful investor and now its greatest philanthropist.

Shortly after I married Warren's son Peter, and long before most of the world outside Wall Street had ever heard of Warren, I visited their family home in Omaha. While there, I met a small group of devoted students of the master investor's wisdom who referred to themselves as Buffettologists. One of the Buffettologists, David Clark, kept notebooks filled with Warren's wisdom on investing, which were meticulous and endlessly fascinating to read. David's notebooks were the foundation upon which he and I later shaped the best-selling investment books *Buffettology, The Buffettology Workbook,* and *The New Buffettology,* now published in ten languages, including Chinese and Russian.

Out of all of David's notebooks, my favorite was filled with many of Warren's most profound aphorisms, which were great fun to read because they had a way of really making you think. As I was later to discover, to Buffettologists, these aphorisms were akin to the teachings of a Taoist master in that the more the student contemplates them, the more they reveal.

As time progressed, I, too, started to collect aphorisms that Warren would say to us in private family moments and at social gatherings that included many business luminaries. At these gatherings, Warren would sometimes take the floor and answer questions in the manner of a master teacher, rewarding the student's patience with his great wisdom.

And the more I heard Warren speak, the more I learned, not only about investing, but about business and life. His aphorisms have a way of staying with you. I often find myself quoting them to make a point or thinking back on them to warn myself not to make a mistake, such as getting swept away in the wild enthusiasm of a bull market. They have even helped teach me what kinds of companies I should focus on and when is the best time to invest in them.

Keeping within the Taoist-like spirit that surrounds Warren's teachings, David and I thought that it would be fun to create *The Tao of Warren Buffett,* filling it with what we think are Warren's most enlightening aphorisms on investing, business management, choosing a career, and pursuing a successful life. These words have been true friends to us over the years as we've navigated our ways through life, business, and the search for the winning investment. We have incorporated our Buffettologists' interpretations to help provide context and to open the door for further exploration into the aphorisms' more hidden and subtle meanings.

It is my hope that this book will enrich your world by making it a more profitable and enjoyable place to invest, work, and live.

Mary Buffett
July 2006

Getting and Staying
Rich

No. 1

"Rule No. 1: Never lose money.
Rule No. 2: Never forget rule No. 1."

✳

The great secret to getting rich is getting your money to compound for you, and the larger sum you start with, all the better. As an example: $100,000 compounding at 15% for twenty years will grow to $1,636,653 in year twenty, which gives you a profit of $1,536,653. But let's say you lost $90,000 of your initial capital before you even started and could only invest $10,000. Your investment would then only grow to $163,665 in year twenty, for a profit of $153,665. This is a much smaller number. The larger the amount of money you lose, the greater the impact on your ability to earn money in the future. That is something that Warren has never forgotten. It is also the reason why he drove an old VW Beetle long after he was a multimillionaire.

No. 2

"I made my first investment at age eleven.
I was wasting my life up until then."

✳

It is good to find one's calling early in life, and in the field of investing it allows for unparalleled opportunities for the magic of compounding sums of money to work. The time to gamble is not when one is young, when there is so much time ahead to profit from wise decisions.

The stock that Warren bought when he was eleven was in an oil company called City Services. He bought three shares at $38, only to watch it sink to $27. He sweated it out and, after it recovered, sold it at $40 a share. Shortly thereafter, it soared to $200 a share and he learned his first lesson in investment—patience. Good things do come to those who wait—provided you pick the right stock.

No. 3

"Never be afraid to ask for too much when
selling or offer too little when buying."

✳

Warren understands that people fear embarrassment if they ask too high a price when selling or offer too low a price when buying. No one wants to be seen as greedy or cheap. Simply stated, in the world of business, how much money you get from a sale or how much you have to pay when making a purchase determines whether you make or lose money and how rich you ultimately become. Once negotiations begin, you can come down in your selling price or up in your buying price. But it's impossible to do the opposite.

Warren has walked from many a deal because it failed to meet his price criteria. Perhaps the most famous example was his Capital Cities purchase of ABC. Warren wanted a larger share of the company for his money than Capital Cities was willing to part with—so he walked from the deal. The next day Capital Cities caved in and gave him the deal he wanted. Ask and you might just receive, but if you don't ask . . .

No. 4

"You can't make a good deal with a bad person."

﹡

A bad person is a bad person, and a bad person will never make you a good deal. The world is filled with enough good and honest people that doing business with the dishonest ones is pure foolishness. If you even have to ask yourself the question "Do I trust this person?" you should immediately leave the negotiating table and look for more honest company with whom to do business. You don't want to doubt that your parachute will open when you are about to jump out of a plane, and you don't want to doubt the integrity of the person with whom you are about to jump into business. If you can't trust them now, you won't be able to trust them later, so why trust them at all?

Warren had this lesson driven home when he was sitting on the board of directors of Salomon Brothers. Against Warren's advice, Salomon's investment bankers continued to do business with media mogul Robert Maxwell, whose finances where so precarious that his nickname was the Bouncing Czech. After Maxwell's untimely demise, Salomon found itself in a big mess trying to recover its money.

The rule is simple: People with integrity are predisposed to perform; people without integrity are predisposed not to perform. It is best not to get the two confused.

No. 5

"The great personal fortunes in this country weren't built on a portfolio of fifty companies. They were built by someone who identified one wonderful business."

✳

If you do a survey of the superrich families in America, you will find that almost without exception their fortunes were built on one exceptional business. The Hearst family made their money in publishing, the Walton family in retailing, the Wrigley family in chewing gum, the Mars family in candy, the Gates family in software, and the Coors and Busch families in brewing. The list goes on and on, and almost without exception, anytime they strayed from that wonderful business that made them so amazingly rich, they ended up losing money—as when Coca-Cola got into the movie business.

The key to Warren's success is that he has been able to identify exactly what the economic characteristics of a wonderful business are—a business that has a durable competitive advantage that owns a piece of the consumer's mind. When you think of gum you think of Wrigley, when think of a discount store you think of Wal-Mart, and when you think of a cold beer you think of Coors or Budweiser. This elevated position creates their economic power. Warren has learned that sometimes the shortsighted nature of the stock market grossly undervalues these wonderful businesses, and when it does he steps up to the plate and buys as many shares as he can. Warren's company, Berkshire Hathaway, is a collection of some of the finest businesses in America, all of which are super profitable and were bought when Wall Street was ignoring them.

No. 6

"It is impossible to unsign a contract, so do all
your thinking before you sign."

✳

Warren has learned that once you sign, the deal is done. You can't
go back and rethink whether it was a good deal or a bad one. So
do all your thinking before you sign. This is easier said than done,
for once that paper is shoved under your nose, sound reasoning
often flies out the window in the name of getting the deal done.
Before signing a contract, imagine all the things that could go
wrong—because they often do go wrong. The road of good inten-
tions is paved with what were foreseeable troubles. Thinking long
and hard before you take the leap will save you from having to
think long and hard about all the trouble you just signed on for.

Warren forgot to put a noncompete clause in his contract with
eighty-nine-year-old Rose Blumkin when he bought her Omaha-
based Nebraska Furniture Mart. A few years later Mrs. B. got
angry at the way things were being done at the store, so she quit
and started up a new store across the street—stealing tons of business from NFM. After a few years of suffering the stiff competition, Warren caved in and agreed to buy her new store for a cool
$5 million. The second time around he had her sign a noncompete
agreement, and it is lucky for him that he did since she continued
on in the business until she was 103.

No. 7

"It is easier to stay out of trouble than
it is to get out of trouble."

✳

It is far easier to avoid the temptation of breaking the law to make easy money than it is to deal with the consequences if you get caught. To stay out of trouble, just do the right thing at the right time. To get out of trouble, you need a lot of money and a lot of legal talent, and even then, you may end up serving a lot of time.

This lesson was driven home when Warren nearly lost his entire $700 million investment in the Wall Street firm of Salomon Brothers. The Federal Reserve Bank came within inches of shutting down the entire firm for its illegal bond-trading activities—which were committed by a trader trying to make a quick buck. What did it cost to get out of trouble? The jobs of several of the firm's top traders, the jobs of its chairman and CEO, and millions in legal fees, fines, lawsuits, and lost business. It would have been a lot easier, and far more profitable, to have stayed out of trouble from the start.

No. 8

"You should invest like a Catholic marries—for life."

❊

Warren knows that if you view an investment decision from the perspective that you will never be able to undo it, you'll be certain to do your homework before taking the plunge. You wouldn't jump into a marriage without doing your research (dating) and discussing it with your advisers (your pals at the pub) and thinking long and hard about it . . . would you? Nor should you jump into an investment without knowing a lot about the company and making sure you understand it. But it is the *life* part that really makes the money. Consider this: In 1973 Warren invested $11 million in the Washington Post Company, and he remains married to this investment even to this day, and over the thirty-three years he has held on to it, it has grown to be worth $1.5 billion. The conviction to stay the course can bring heavenly rewards, as long as you have chosen the right one to begin with.

No. 9

"Wall Street is the only place that people ride to in a Rolls-Royce to get advice from those who take the subway."

✳

Warren has always thought it strange that highly successful and intelligent businesspeople, who have spent lifetimes making huge sums of money, will take investment advice from stockbrokers too poor to take their own advice. And if their advice is so great, why aren't they all rich? Maybe it's because they don't get rich off their advice but off charging you commissions? One should beware of people who need to use your money to make you rich, especially when the more things they sell you means the more money they will make. More often than not, their agenda is to use your money to make themselves rich. And if they lose your money? Well, they just go out and find someone else to sell their advice to.

Warren feels so strongly about where Wall Street's true loyalties lie that he refuses to even look at the business projections that its analysts put together because, regardless of the nature of the business, the projections are always way too rosy.

No. 10

"Happiness does not buy you money."

＊

Warren never confused being rich with happiness. We are talking about a guy who still hangs out with the same people he did in high school and still lives in the same neighborhood in which he grew up. Money hasn't changed who he is on a fundamental level. When asked by college students to define success, he has said it is being loved by the people you hope love you. You can be the richest man in the world, but without the love of family and friends, you would also be the poorest.

No. 11

"It takes twenty years to build a reputation and
five minutes to lose it. If you think about that,
you will do things differently."

✳

One foolish act and the bad press that goes with it can instantly destroy a good reputation that has taken a lifetime to build. It's best not to do something that you know is wrong, because if you are caught, the price you pay may be more than you can afford. This is a Buffett credo that he whispered into the ears of his children from the time they were tots.

When the accounting scandal came down with insurance giant AIG, Buffett told his managers, "The current investigation of the insurance industry underscores the imperative of the message that I regularly send to you in my biannual memo: Berkshire can afford to lose money, even lots of money; it can't afford to lose reputation, even a shred of reputation. . . . And in the long run we will have whatever reputation we deserve. There is plenty of money to be made in the center of the court. There is no need to play around the edges."

Wall Street is littered with fallen giants who let greed get in the way of good judgment and failed to heed this advice.

No. 12

"The market, like the Lord, helps those who help themselves. But unlike the Lord, the market does not forgive those who know not what they do."

✳

The stock market is there to make you rich if you know what you are doing. But if you don't know what you are doing, it will show no mercy in making you poor. Ignorance, when mixed with greed, is the stuff financial disasters are made of. In 1969, at the high end of the sixties bull market, Warren thought stocks were so overpriced that he got out of the market completely. By 1973–74 the stock market had completely reversed itself and stocks were selling at bargain prices. Warren bought them up with the appetite of, as he said, "a sex-starved man in the middle of a harem filled with beautiful women." Many of those beauties went on to help make him a billionaire.

As for those investors who stayed in the market after Warren left in 1969, many of them lost their shirts when it crashed in '73–74, and getting back in became impossible—you need money to buy stocks. It really does help if you know what you are doing.

No. 13

"I don't try to jump over seven-foot bars;
I look around for one-foot bars that I can step over."

✳

Warren isn't shooting for the stars. He isn't trying to hit home runs on every pitch. He is waiting for the perfect pitch and is staying with the sure thing: companies with products that don't have to change, businesses that he knows will still be around in twenty years, selling now at a price that would make business sense even if he were buying the whole company. Lucky for him that the short-term focus of the stock market often neglects the long-term economics of a business, which means the stock market will often misprice a great business. He keeps it simple and leaves all the fortune-telling and complex investment strategies to the other guys on Wall Street.

In the stock market crash of 1973–74 you could buy Ogilvy & Mather, one of the strongest advertising agencies in the world, for $4 a share against per share earnings of $.76, which equated to a P/E of 5. Warren bought a ton of it during the crash and cashed out many years later after an annual rate of return of better than 20%. Some investments are just that simple.

No. 14

"The chains of habit are too light to be felt
until they are too heavy to be broken."

＊

This is Warren quoting the English philosopher Bertrand Russell, because his words so aptly describe the insidious nature of bad business habits that don't become apparent until it is too late. Such as cost cutting after your business is in trouble, which should've been done long before you even got to the doorsteps of danger. The business that becomes bloated with unnecessary expenses in times of plenty is the business that will sink when things turn for the worse. This propensity to delude oneself also tells you a lot about the management that let the business become bloated with expenses in the first place. It is best to consciously check where all your habits are taking you long before you get there. If you don't like the direction in which you are headed, the time to change course is before you find your ship sinking in a sea of troubles.

This is what happened to Warren with the Benjamin Graham–inspired investment strategy of buying bargain stocks that were selling below book value regardless of the nature of the company's long-term economics. This was something Warren was able to do with great success during the 1950s and early 1960s. But he stayed with this approach long after it wasn't viable anymore—the chains of habit were too light to be felt. When he finally woke up in the late 1970s to the fact that the Graham bargain ride was over, he shifted over to a strategy of buying exceptional businesses at reasonable prices and then holding them for long periods—thereby letting the business grow in value. With the old strategy he made millions, but with the new one he made billions.

No. 15

"Marrying for money is probably a bad idea
under any circumstances, but it is
absolutely nuts if you are already rich."

✳

The wise know that if you marry for money, you will earn every penny of it. So if you are already rich, why on earth would you want to work that hard! It is easier to marry for love and make the money later. It is what Warren did with his wife, Susie—they found love and then they went out and made a fortune. Besides, the couple that makes money together is often the couple that stays together. And if they don't stay together, at least they have a ton of money to fight over. (Warren is silent on the wisdom of divorce.)

No. 16

"It's not necessary to do extraordinary things
to get extraordinary results."

✳

As an investor you don't have to try to get rich overnight to eventually get rich. Warren is shooting for a 20% annual rate of return, not a 200% annual rate of return. Invest $100,000 for twenty years at 20% a year and you end up with $3.8 million; hold it for thirty years and you end up with $23.7 million. You win with the running game—not the long bomb. With a world trying to get an annual return of 100%, a lot of mistakes are being made regarding long-term business economics that make getting a 20% annual return pretty easy.

No. 17

"You should look at stocks as
small pieces of a business."

✳

Sometimes when people invest, they forget that they are actually buying a fractional interest in a business. Warren likes to look at stocks as owning a small piece of a business. This way he can judge whether he is paying too much for the business. He multiplies the stock price by the number of shares outstanding, then asks himself whether this would be a good deal or a bad deal if he were buying the whole business. If the price is too rich to be buying the whole business, then it is too rich to be buying even a single share. This thought alone can stop you from foolishly getting caught in the speculative frenzy that often goes with a bull market, for seldom do Wall Street darlings and other fashionable securities sell at prices at which it would make sense to buy the whole business.

No. 18

"My idea of a group decision is to look in the mirror."

＊

Warren is not one to seek affirmation of his ideas from others, because so many of his ideas are the opposite of what the herd is thinking. To make big money in the investment world you have to learn to think independently; to think independently you need to be comfortable standing alone.

Warren has a history of standing alone that dates back to the early days of his investment career. He chose to live in Omaha instead of NYC because there was less influence from Wall Street. He bought into Berkshire Hathaway when no one wanted it; he bought into American Express when no one wanted it; he bought into the Washington Post Company when no one wanted it; he bought into General Foods when no one wanted it; he bought into RJR Tobacco when no one wanted it; he bought into GEICO when no one wanted it; he bought the bonds of the Washington Public Power Supply System when no one wanted them; and he bought into junk bonds when no one wanted them. Some of these investments he still owns, some of them he sold after holding them a number of years, but on each and every one of them he made a fortune. If he had taken a vote of confidence from anyone on Wall Street, he would have missed the boat on all these great investments.

No. 19

"If I can't make money in a $5 trillion U.S. market,
it may be a little bit of wishful thinking to think that
all I have to do is get a few thousand miles offshore
and I'll start showing my stuff."

✳

The odd thing about this quote is that ten years later Warren did go offshore to show his stuff. In 2003 he bought around $500 million worth of PetroChina, an oil company that is 90% owned by the Chinese government, which means, as Warren jokingly remarked, "Between the two of us we control the company." PetroChina is the fourth most profitable oil company in the world. It produces as much crude as Exxon, and Warren bought it at one-third the valuation of Western oil companies. In case you are wondering, it is up 400% since then. And if that's not showing your stuff, I don't know what is.

No. 20

"You should invest in a business that even a fool
can run, because someday a fool will."

✳

There are businesses with great underlying economics and businesses with poor underlying economics. You want to invest in companies with great underlying economics because it is hard to damage these kinds of businesses. Companies in which Warren has invested, such as Coca-Cola, Budweiser, Wal-Mart, Wrigley's, Hershey, and H&R Block, are almost dumbproof. You know you are going to make money with these businesses, even if a fool becomes CEO. But if you have to worry about a fool running the business, then maybe it isn't such a great business, and maybe you shouldn't be in it.

No. 21

"With each investment you make, you should have the
courage and the conviction to place at least 10%
of your net worth in that stock."

✳

Conviction is based on what you know will happen; faith is based
on what you hope will happen. To make money in the investment
game you need to have conviction, which means that you need to
know what you are doing. A surefire way to achieve Warren's level
of conviction is to invest significant amounts of money. This causes
you to focus and make certain that you have done your homework
before you make your investment. But if your investment strategy
is based on faith, then you really haven't a prayer.

No. 22

"Money, to some extent, sometimes lets you be in more interesting environments. But it can't change how many people love you or how healthy you are."

✳

The truth is that excessively large amounts of money can actually create a great deal of misery in your life. Your children won't work because they think they are going to inherit a fortune, which means that they never develop any of the self-esteem that work creates, which means that they end up being bitter and spending their time wishing you an early demise. If you are insanely rich, you may end up being surrounded by a bunch of sycophants who will fill your life with lies to stoke your illusions of grandeur till you look like a fool to the rest of the world. And instead of doing adventurous things with your money and life, you end up spending all your time guarding your wealth from your servants, lawyers, accountants, and so-called money managers, all of whom will assist you in making your money theirs.

Warren believes that children who inherit great wealth tend to do nothing with their lives, nor does he believe that it is good for society if there is an upper class created by inherited wealth. He believes that a country prospers better if society is a meritocracy, with people earning what they get. For this reason he donated the $32 billion fortune he made from investing to charity, so that it would go back to help the very society that created it. Let this noble thought find a place in the hearts of all who make their fortunes in the world.

Business

No. 23

"Anything that can't go on forever will end."

✳

A stock price that is quickly rising will stop rising when the economic reality of the business finally sets in. It might seem as if it can go on forever, but if the business fails to perform up to the expectations that are driving the rising price, the company's shares will peak and then drop like a brick.

Most businesses that are doing well now will, at some future point, do poorly. Things change—it is only a matter of time. Buggy whips were at one time a great business in America, video players were once the rage, selling and fixing typewriters a necessary and intricate part of the commercial equation. Now they are just things of the past with no economic promise whatsoever. Things do end, which is why you not only have to keep your eye on the ball, but also on the road ahead.

Several times Warren has invested in businesses that either came to an end or saw a radical decline under his stewardship. The most notable were Blue Chip Stamps, which all but vanished, and World Book Encyclopedia, which is now vanishing, each of which lost out to a changing business environment that the company was powerless to make money in. Even a genius can misread the road ahead.

No. 24

"When management with a reputation for brilliance
tackles a business with a reputation for poor
fundamental economics, it is the reputation of
the business that remains intact."

＊

There are great businesses—with great underlying economics—that
have the financial wherewithal to turn themselves around when
they get into trouble. And there are mediocre businesses—with
poor underlying economics—that are impossible to save regardless
of the brilliance of managers. A great business is usually awash in
cash, carries little or no debt, and is in a great position to either buy
its way out of trouble or ride out any downturn in the economy.
Mediocre businesses are always struggling for cash and are loaded
with debt, and if they get into problems, they usually have to rob
Peter to pay Paul, which leads to even more problems. No matter
how brilliantly a mediocre business is run, its poor inherent economics will keep it forever anchored to poor results.

No. 25

"Accounting is the language of business."

＊

There are many ways to describe what is going on with a business, but whatever is said, it always comes back to the language of accounting. When Warren was asked by the daughter of one his business associates what courses she should study in college, he replied, "Accounting—it is the language of business." To read a company's financial statement you need to know how to read the numbers. To do that you need to learn accounting. If you can't read the scorecard, you can't keep score, which means that you can't tell the winners from the losers.

No. 26

"Turnarounds seldom turn."

✳

The world is full of businesses with poor economics selling at what seem to be bargain prices. Warren looks for a good business that is selling at a fair price, or even better, a great business at a bargain price (which is hard to find). Poor businesses remain poor businesses regardless of the price you pay for them. The price of the stock may change, but the underlying character of the business tends to remain the same. If it is a good business, it will remain a good business, and if it is a bad business, it will remain a bad business. Bad businesses can't be turned into great businesses. Only in fairy tales do frogs turn into princes, and although many CEOs believe that they have the power of the magic kiss, 95% of the frogs they kiss remain frogs—and the 5% that do turn around probably weren't frogs to begin with. Warren believes that the same managerial energy and capital would be better spent buying a business with good economics that is selling at a fair price, than on taking on a poor business in need of a magic kiss, even if it is selling at a bargain price. After kissing a few frogs in his life, he concluded that they don't taste very good.

No. 27

"If a business does well, the stock eventually follows."

✳

A market phenomenon that Warren relies on is that if the underlying business does well over a long period of time, the stock price will increase to reflect the underlying increase in the value of the company. Likewise, if the underlying business does not do well over a long period of time, the stock price will decrease to better reflect the underlying value of the company. The long-term value of the company has a way of rectifying the situation, no matter which direction. Thus, Internet stocks that saw their prices soar skywards during the bull market saw them drop like a rock when they failed to make any money over the long run. Likewise, great companies that saw their stock prices plummet in the stock market crash saw them immediately recover once the market saw that their earning power had remained intact.

If you buy a stock that has had its price beaten down, you'd better make sure that the long-term economics of the business are still good. If they are, and the business does well over the long term, so will the stock. For the stock price to improve, the business must do well, and to do well it helps immensely if it was a great business to begin with. The Washington Post Company, Coca-Cola, Disney, American Express, General Foods, Wells Fargo, Interpublic Group, and GEICO were all companies that had excellent economics working in their favor at the time that Warren bought into them, but had stock prices that were suffering from either a one-time solvable problem or an industry recession or a bear market. With every single one of these companies the long-term economics they possessed eventually caused the stock market to revalue their stock prices handsomely upward.

No. 28

"Managing your career is like investing—the degree
of difficulty does not count. So you can save yourself
money and pain by getting on the right train."

✳

One not only needs to learn what kind of business to invest in but
what kind to work in. If one goes to work for a company with poor
long-term economics, then he can never expect to do really well
because the company doesn't do well. Salaries will be below average and raises will be few and long between, and there is greater
risk of losing your job because management will always be under
pressure to cut costs.

But if you go to work for a company that has great long-term
economics working in its favor, then the company will be awash in
cash. This means higher salaries and tons of raises and promotions
for a job well done. Plus there will be plenty of room for advance-
ment as management looks for ways to spend all that free cash.

You want to work for a company that has high margins and
makes lots of money. And you want to stay away from businesses
that have low margins and lose money. One is a first-class train ride
to Easy Street; the other is a long, slow, hard freight-train ride to
a Siberian nowhere.

No. 29

"The reaction of weak management to weak
operations is often weak accounting."

✳

If the business has lousy economics working against it, and the
management lacks integrity, it will support weak accounting, which
manifests itself by creating earnings where there really aren't any.
This is very, very easy to do—just book a cost as an investment in
a partnership, then have the partnership pay you a fee out of the
money you invested in it, which you book as income. Reduce costs
and increase income with just a few strokes of a pen. The increase
in earnings will get the shareholders and Wall Street to applaud
you, which will cause the stock price to rise, which will get you a
big juicy bonus worth millions and an invitation to have lunch with
the president. Just think Enron, but there are others. . . .

No. 30

"There is a huge difference between the business that grows and requires lots of capital to do so and the business that grows and doesn't require capital."

✳

This is the big secret in Warren's buy-and-hold-forever strategy. If you buy and hold a business that requires lots of capital to grow, your stock is never going to grow in value. The reason is the constant drain of capital just to keep the business from sinking in the wake of competition. If you have to spend billions redesigning your product mix every five years, those are billions that can't be spent expanding operations or buying new businesses or buying back stock. But a business that can grow without new infusions of capital can afford to spend its excess cash doing those things, all of which will increase the company's per share earnings, which will, in turn, cause the company's stock price to increase. This is why Warren prefers companies like Wrigley's and Coca-Cola as opposed to GM or Intel. Companies like Wrigley's and Coca-Cola never have to spend billions redesigning their product or retooling their manufacturing plants, which leaves them plenty of money to spend on such fun things as buying back their own stock. GM and Intel, on the other hand, have to constantly spend billions on new designs and retooling. If either one stopped spending billions on new designs or retooling, it would be put out of business by its competition. If a business needs lots of capital to grow, it will never make you rich, and if it doesn't need lots of capital to grow, it won't ever leave you poor.

No. 31

"In a difficult business, no sooner is one problem
solved than another surfaces—never is there
just one cockroach in the kitchen."

✳

A business with poor economics is a slow boat to nowhere and
makes a lousy long-term investment. The intensely competitive
nature of the business means that it will suffer slim margins on sales
and have a constant need to upgrade the plant to stay competitive.
If its products have to constantly change to stay competitive, then
there is the added problem of financing research and development.
For example, if a company that manufactures autos decides to
change its line of products, it is going to have to spend billions
retooling. One wrong guess and it might just bankrupt the entire
operation. All of these things drain capital that could be spent to
increase earnings, such as expanding operations, buying new businesses, or repurchasing stock. These constant crises of poor margins and poor earnings mean a constant battle with costs, and if
you add in competition from overseas labor, you may find yourself
in a business that is no longer operationally viable in its present
form. In the game of long-term investing these are the kinds of
businesses that you want to stay away from. Warren avoids them
like the plague, even if the stock market is giving them away.

No. 32

"You can always juice sales by going down-market,
but it's hard to go back upmarket."

＊

Certain products own a piece of your mind—they are the brand-name products that you think of when you have a particular need. Kleenex, Tampax, Windex, Snickers, Wrigley's, Disney, and Coke are all brands that own a piece of the consumer's mind. Along with owning a piece of the consumer's mind goes a set of consumer expectations regarding that product. And because these products all meet those expectations, their manufacturers can charge a higher price for fulfilling the consumer's needs. Manufacturers will spend millions on getting their products to this vaunted status.

However, if a manufacturer, in the name of increasing profits, decreases the quality of its products, it can run a huge risk of losing its ownership of the consumer's mind. We have all seen this happen—a quality product we love to use, but then the manufacturer cheapens it and we stop using it. Once this happens, it is hard for the manufacturer to go back, because the bad experience with the product now owns a piece of the consumer's mind.

No. 33

"When a chief executive officer is encouraged by his advisers to make deals, he responds much as would a teenage boy who is encouraged by his father to have a normal sex life. It's not a push he needs."

✳

As Blaise Pascal, an influential French mathematician and philosopher, once said, "All man's miseries derive from not being able to sit quietly in a room alone." CEOs can't sit quietly; they are predisposed to make deals, which are made easy to do by Wall Street, and create the illusion that they are doing something to justify their incredibly high salaries. Besides, it is often easier to buy a new set of problems than it is to try to fix an old set. Warren's solution to this raging appetite to grow through acquisitions is to only buy companies that have some kind of durable competitive advantage. These companies have great underlying economics working for them as evidenced by high returns on equity and strong and consistent earnings. The other kinds of companies he has labeled commodity-type businesses, which are evidenced by low returns on equity and erratic earnings. Since most of the companies in the world fall into the commodity type, it is easy for Warren to find some rest—but when a company shows up with a durable competitive advantage, he jumps on it ten minutes after he sees the deal. Warren knows what he wants before he wants it.

No. 34

"You don't have to make money back the
same way you lost it."

✳

Beginning investors sometimes think that the only game in town is the stock they just lost money on, so they keep playing it, as if it's a game in a casino, hoping that their luck will change. But with stocks, unlike casino games of chance, the risk varies dramatically from one stock to another, all of it based largely on two factors— the quality of the company and the price you pay for its shares in relation to that quality. The higher the quality, the lower the risk, and the lower the price in relation to the quality of the business, the lower the risk. Most of the time high quality comes with a high price, which is not that good a deal, but occasionally the stock market does something freaky and you get high quality selling at a low price. This is where the easy money is made. What you want to stay away from is low-quality businesses selling at a high price, because that is where fortunes are lost. Low quality and a high price in relation to the quality of the business means stay away, and high quality and a low price in relation to the quality of the business means come play. But every single stock is a new game, with new odds, which change as the price of the stock changes, so wait till you find one where the odds are so much in your favor that you have a margin of safety, then bet big. The funny thing about the stock market is that, unlike a casino, it occasionally serves up a sure thing. Warren is all about the sure thing.

No. 35

"I look for businesses in which I think I can predict what they're going to look like in ten to fifteen years' time. Take Wrigley's chewing gum. I don't think the Internet is going to change how people chew gum."

*

Consistent products equal consistent earnings. If the product doesn't have to change, you can reap all the benefits of not having to spend money on research and development, nor do you have to fall victim to the ups and downs of fashion. Think beer, soda pop, and candy. Budweiser has been making the same brew for over a hundred years, Coke has been selling the same magical caramel-colored sugar water for over a hundred years, and Wrigley's has been making the same chewing gum for, you guessed it, over a hundred years. Catching the trend here? Do you think you can predict what these companies will probably be selling in fifteen years? If you can, then you might just be the next Warren Buffett.

Warren's Mentors

No. 36

"Someone is sitting in the shade today because
someone planted a tree a long time ago."

✳

If not for the hard work of Warren's mentor Benjamin Graham in developing the concept of value investing, Warren might never have gotten out from behind the counter at his grandfather's grocery store. For it is easy to become brilliant at what you do when you stand on the shoulders of a giant—the trick is picking the right giant. In Warren's case, he chose Graham, a man known as the Dean of Wall Street. Graham developed the concept of value investing and taught a course on it at Columbia University in NYC. Warren took Graham's course, and in the words of his classmate Bill Ruane, "Sparks were flying between the two." After Columbia, Warren went to work at Graham's Wall Street investment firm, and the rest of the story is the stuff of which financial legends are made.

No. 37

"With enough inside information and a million dollars,
you can go broke in a year."

∗

Face it, by the time inside information gets to you, everyone else
has heard it and traded on it. Besides, trading on inside informa-
tions is against the law. Warren has often said that one of the
advantages to living in Omaha is that no one's around to whisper
inside scoops in his ear over lunch. Often, unscrupulous types start
rumors so that they can drive up the price of shares so that they
can dump them in the laps of gullible investors. Famed 1920s
investment great Bernard Baruch was famous for selling out a
stock position as soon as someone gave him a hot tip on it. Baruch,
by the way, died a very, very rich man.

No. 38

"Read Ben Graham and Phil Fisher, read annual reports,
but don't do equations with Greek letters in them."

✳

Ben Graham taught that you should only buy a stock when it is selling at a low price in relationship to its long-term value. The low price will give you a margin of safety against calamity. Phil Fisher said that you need to buy a high-quality company, then hold it for a long, long time and let the retained earnings build up the value. Warren took Ben's "buy at a low price to get a margin of safety" and married it to Phil's "buy the highest-quality company and hold it forever" and ended up with "buy high-quality companies at low prices in relation to their value and then hold them for a long, long time." This is one of those equations where the sum is greater than its parts. Warren ended up making far more money than either Ben or Phil, who were the master investors of their day. As far as the equations with Greek letters in them are concerned, they are for the Wall Street types who didn't get around to reading Ben and Phil.

No. 39

"I am a better investor because I am a businessman,
and a better businessman because I am an investor."

＊

A smart businessman knows a good business from a bad one—and
a smart investor knows when a business is being sold cheap or is
overpriced. So to be great at investing you need to be like the businessman and know a good business from a bad one, and when you
go to buy a business, you need to be like the smart investor and
know whether it is selling cheap or it is overpriced. Combine the
two and you can make a billion. It's that easy, and it's that hard.

In Warren's early days he was only concerned with the histori-
cal financials of a company, he didn't really care about the products
it produced. His mentor Graham believed the numbers reflected
everything there was to know; he didn't separate a commodity-type
business such as textiles, which has poor long-term economics, from
a consumer-monopoly business such as Coke, which has great long-
term economics. But as Warren became active in running a struggling commodity-type business, he soon realized that it was the
consumer-monopoly-type companies that had the competitive
advantage and were producing the superior results. Graham would
buy anything as long as it was cheap. Warren will only buy a consumer-monopoly-type company that has a competitive advantage,
and he doesn't have to wait for it to be selling cheap. A fair price is
all he needs, if he holds on to it long enough, to make his billions.

No. 40

"If principles become dated,
they're no longer principles."

※

Warren woke up one morning and discovered that the investment principles he had learned from his teacher Graham were no longer useful. Graham had advocated buying cheap companies regardless of the underlying economics of the business. This strategy worked well in the forties and fifties, but it lost its effectiveness as a larger group of investors began to practice this kind of investing—it got harder and harder to find the golden eggs. Instead of staying the course, Warren jumped ship and adopted a philosophy of investing in exceptional companies that had a durable competitive advantage, as long as they were selling at reasonable prices—then he would let the rising waters of time and earnings lift the price of the stock. This new philosophy lifted him from being rich to being superrich.

An excellent example of this was his investment in Coca-Cola, for which he paid approximately twenty times earnings. The old Warren would never have made this investment because the Grahamian valuation techniques would have deemed it way too pricey. But for the new Warren it was a more-than-fair price that paid off for him in the billions. Sometimes it is a good thing if a leopard can change his spots.

No. 41

"You pay a very high price in the stock market
for a cheery consensus."

✳

If everyone agrees with you that a particular stock is the next Microsoft, you are going to have to pay a steep price—which leaves little upside and lots of downside. What you want is to find a stock that no one is looking at or that is out of favor with the big investment funds and is selling at a low price relative to its long-term economic value. Many that have risen shall fall, and many that have fallen shall rise again. This was the battle cry of Warren's mentor Benjamin Graham. We are interested in the rise-again part—we do not want to be paying sky-high prices for stocks that are just waiting to fall—we want to be paying bargain prices for stocks that are waiting to rise.

Education

No. 42

"If calculus or algebra were required to be a great investor,
I'd have to go back to delivering newspapers."

✳

According to Warren, the math skills you need to be a great investor
are addition, subtraction, multiplication, division, and the ability
to rapidly calculate percentages and probability. Anything more, as
the French would say, is a waste. Anything less and you can't play
the game.

No.43

"You have to think for yourself. It always amazes me
how high-IQ people mindlessly imitate. I never
get good ideas talking to other people."

✳

Many high-IQ types think that the way to get rich is to imitate
others. This is in part due to an education system that rewards imitating the professor. On Wall Street the dominant investment strategy is based on imitating what the herd is doing—it is easier to sell
you something that is popular as opposed to something that is
unpopular. Warren isn't trying to sell anyone investments—he's
just trying to get rich off investments. This is done not by follow-
ing the herd, but by identifying stocks that Wall Street doesn't want
today, but will be dying for tomorrow. As for those who follow the
herd—well, they usually spend a lot of time scraping their shoes.

No. 44

"The smarter the journalists are,
the better off society is."

＊

We get our information for processing investment ideas from the media, which means we are wholly dependent on journalists for accuracy and proper analysis of what is going on. Do you want dumb people keeping us informed, or do you want intelligent people doing the job? Warren has always subscribed to the idea that the better the teacher, the smarter the student body. Thus, the smarter the journalists, the smarter the society. The only people who don't want a smarter society are liars, thieves, and politicians who are trying to hide something.

No. 45

"You want to learn from experience, but you want to
learn from other people's experience when you can."

*

Experience is the best teacher, but it can be expensive if you are
learning from your own mistakes. It is better to learn from the mistakes of others. This is why Warren has made it part of his educa-
tional diet to study and dissect the business and investing mistakes
of others. He wants to learn where they went wrong so he doesn't
go there. This is a completely opposite strategy from that of most
business schools, which study only success stories. In business and
in investing, more people end up in the gutter than on Easy Street—
you need to study not only what to do, but what not to do.

The Workplace

No. 46

"It's hard to teach a young dog old tricks."

＊

Warren has found that the business acumen that comes with age is next to impossible to teach to younger managers. The old birds have got it wired and know how to make a buck. Warren is in his seventies, his partner Charlie Munger is in his eighties, Mrs. B. ran the Nebraska Furniture Mart at over one hundred, and many of the managers at Berkshire Hathaway, Warren's holding company, have stayed on well into their seventies. Warren has no mandatory retirement age at Berkshire. In Warren's world, sixty-five is just getting started—age and experience can be far greater virtues than youth and enthusiasm when it comes to making money the old-fashioned way.

No. 47

"In looking for someone to hire, you look for three qualities: integrity, intelligence, and energy. But the most important is integrity, because if they don't have that, the other two qualities, intelligence and energy, are going to kill you."

※

When you hire someone to run your business, you are entrusting him or her with the piggy bank. If these people are smart and hard-working, they are going to make you a lot of money, but if they aren't honest, they will find lots of clever ways to make all your money theirs. So if you have to hire people who aren't honest, make sure they're not hardworking and are dumb as bricks—that way all they will be able to steal are the bricks.

Integrity is the key ingredient to Warren's management philosophy. When he bought the Nebraska Furniture Mart from Mrs. B., he surprised her and the rest of the Mart's management by not requesting an audit of her books. He simply asked her what it was worth, and she told him, and the next day he brought her a check for $40 million. When Mrs. B. asked him about it later, he replied that he trusted her far more than he trusted his accountants.

Also, Warren's management style has always been to afford his managers tremendous operational autonomy. They are free to run the businesses as if they are the owners. He couldn't give his managers this much freedom if they lacked integrity.

No. 48

"Can you really explain to a fish what it is like to walk on land? One day on land is worth a thousand years talking about it, and one day running a business has exactly the same kind of value."

✳

As they say in the military, it's all fun and games until someone starts shooting back. The same applies to the business world. Dealing with real manufacturing problems and getting and keeping real customers is what separates the academics from the managerial real world. At the Berkshire-owned Nebraska Furniture Mart in Omaha, company founder and top manager, Mrs. B., rode to business victory after victory, decade upon decade, with the frontline troops at the Mart. Age and experience before youth and enthusiasm has become Warren's battle cry that makes Berkshire's cash register ring and ring and ring. . . .

No. 49

"It's only when the tide goes out that you learn
who's been swimming naked."

✳

Creative accounting has let more than a few of Wall Street's darlings rise to the top. But if the real money doesn't show up at some point, the enthusiasm and illusion fall away, and all that is left is an empty bank account and a bankruptcy filing. The tide went out on Enron and we all saw that the emperor had no clothes. The problem is finding out who is swimming naked before the tide goes out.

No. 50

"When ideas fail, words come in very handy."

✳

This is Warren quoting Goethe, and what he means by this is that when your great idea blows apart and you lose the business, you will use words to conjure a great excuse so you won't look as if you're incompetent. In the world of CEOs there is a never-ending quest for good excuses to soothe irate shareholders' anger over management's poor decisions. By not taking the blame they are essentially saying that the buck doesn't stop here. If it doesn't stop with the CEO, then he must not really be our leader, right? If he isn't our leader, then why don't we go out and get ourselves some-one who can lead to run our business? It is our business, isn't it? We are the owners, right? Warren has never forgotten that Berkshire's shareholders own the business that he runs. That is why he is always forthcoming, not only about the good news, but also the bad.

No. 51

"The really good business manager doesn't wake up
in the morning and say, 'This is the day that I am
going to cut costs,' any more than he wakes up
and decides to practice breathing."

✳

The time to get your vaccinations is not the day after you contract
the disease. In the business world, much of managing is done reac-
tively. Warren believes in proactive management—fixing the potential problem before it becomes a problem. You keep costs low from
the start, which keeps more powder dry for an attack by your competitors and creates more profits when things are good. Warren
staffs Berkshire's home office with a lean, mean office machine of
seventeen. Here is a man who practices what he preaches. If you
read that a company is instigating a cost-cutting program, then you
know that management has been slacking in keeping costs low from
the start. What do you think of a company with management that
does not have a grip on costs? Do you think they are going to make
their shareholders a lot of money?

No. 52

"Wouldn't it be great if we could buy love for $1 million.
But the only way to be loved is to be lovable. You
always get back more than you give away. If you don't
give any, you won't get any. There's nobody I know who
commands the love of others who doesn't feel like a
success. And I can't imagine people who aren't
loved feel very successful."

＊

Love is important in Warren's personal life and he has incorporated it into his business and management philosophy. He only
hires people who love what they are doing, because if you love
what you are doing, you will treat others well so that they will, in
turn, also love what they do. He never degrades his managers
when they make mistakes. Rather, he encourages them not to dwell
on mistakes and to get on with business. His love and respect for
his managers is so strong that he trusts them completely with the
businesses they run. He gives them complete control over them,
which promotes a strong sense of responsibility. Warren talks endlessly about how proud he is of his management teams and never
hesitates to sing their praises in public. This is how he is able to
attract the best and the brightest managers in the world. Love and
respect really do beget love and respect; it's the first step on the
road to being a success in life.

No. 53

"We enjoy the process far more than the proceeds,
though I have learned to live with those also."

✳

People who are passionate about their jobs will come to rule their
trade or profession because they love the process more than the
money. The funny thing about passion is that money usually follows it. People who love money more than their work spend their
lives working in misery and usually end up earning much less than
if they had followed their heart in the first place. The greatest thing
about being passionate about your work is that it really isn't a job;
it's fun. Warren has always said that he loves what he does so much
that he would pay to have his job. But he doesn't have to because
he makes a ton of money doing what he loves.

No. 54

"If you hit a hole in one on every hole,
you wouldn't play golf for very long."

✳

A job with challenges keeps things interesting, creates high self-esteem, promotes creativity, and attracts the highest-quality people. A job without challenges is boring, creates low self-esteem, and attracts the least-motivated people. However, for challenges to be present, there also has to be risk. In the world of business, as challenges arise, decisions have to be made, and inevitably mistakes will happen. It is the nature of making decisions and it is also what makes it all so interesting. Warren has learned that if he wants to attract the best and brightest managers, the ones who are self-motivated and aggressive in taking on challenges, then he must give them a work environment that will allow them to make the mistakes that come along with the successes.

No. 55

"There comes a time when you ought to start doing what you want. Take a job that you love. You will jump out of bed in the morning. I think you are out of your mind if you keep taking jobs that you don't like because you think that it will look good on your résumé. Isn't that a little like saving up sex for your old age?"

＊

Spending a life getting up and going to a job that you hate, with people that you don't respect, leads to frustration and discontent, which you bring home with you from work and share with your family, which makes them unhappy as well. This, of course, makes for a lousy life for everyone you love, including yourself. It is much better to find a job that you love. Then, going to work puts a smile on your face, which you can take home with you at the end of the day to share with your loved ones. And if you are worried about money, keep in mind that the people who love what they are doing are the ones who rise to the top of their fields and end up making the most money, be it the poor Russian immigrant who couldn't read but loved to sell furniture or the nerdy son of a grocery clerk who had a thing for numbers and stocks. Do what you love and the money will come. It worked for them and it will work for you.

No. 56

"A friend of mine spent twenty years looking for the perfect woman; unfortunately, when he found her, he discovered that she was looking for the perfect man."

✳

What Warren's friend failed to realize is that selling someone on what you have is different from buying what someone else has. He was sold on her goods, but she wasn't sold on his. In life and in business you have to sell the other person on who you are and what you have for them to buy. Warren had to sell himself to his original investors, and he still has to sell himself to the privately held family businesses that Berkshire wants to buy—people who have spent their lives building a business aren't interested in selling "their baby" to just anybody. Warren sells them on the idea that he will give those businesses a good home. In our daily lives we have to sell ourselves to our employers and to our customers. Business relationships are just like personal relationships—they are best started by showing an interest in the other person, and in finding out what that person's needs are, because ultimately we are selling to those needs. He or she who forgets that will spend a lot of time sitting alone at the bar.

Analysts, Advisers,
Brokers—Follies to Avoid

No. 57

"Never ask a barber if you need a haircut."

✳

Ask an adviser if there is a problem and he will find a problem—
even if there isn't one. Warren found this to be true of investment
bankers, management advisers, lawyers, auto mechanics, lawn-care
consultants, and the like. People who are paid to fix problems will
always find problems because if there isn't a problem, there is nothing to fix.

No. 58

"Forecasts usually tell us more of the forecaster
than of the forecast."

✳

What most people forget is that most forecasters have an agenda
that reflects the interests of the people who are paying their
salary—if they are being paid to be pessimistic, they will be
pessimistic; if optimism is needed, then it is optimism you will get.
People are what they are being paid to be—no more, no less. Forecasters don't have a crystal ball that they can see into the future
with, but they do have mortgages that need servicing and children
who need to go to college. Wall Street likes to see a lot of trading
activity, and that means it needs reasons to make a lot of changes
to your investment portfolio. If the forecaster says interest rates
are going up, you sell your stocks; if he says rates are going down,
you buy stocks. They do the same thing with individual stocks—
predict lower earnings this quarter and you are selling out, predict
higher earnings this quarter and you are buying in. Wall Street
makes its money off your moving around your money from one
investment to another, so, naturally, Wall Street forecasters, also
known as analysts, are going to find lots of reasons for you to do
just that, move from one investment to another. The problem is
that all this activity has nothing to do with making you rich.

No. 59

"A public-opinion poll is no substitute for thought."

✳

There is a great deal of comfort when you invest with the crowd. Everyone agrees with you. However, when you invest with the crowd, you have to worry about when the crowd will leave the party, because, just like in high school, no one stays popular forever. There usually isn't much upside potential left in a stock after it becomes really popular, which means you took on a lot of risk for a shot at a low rate of return. If you are a thinking investor, like Warren, you look for stocks that are going through an unpopular phase, because that is where you are going to find tomorrow's Mr. Popular selling at a discount price, which equates to a low risk of losing your money and great potential for a high rate of return.

No. 60

"The business schools reward difficult,
complex behavior more than simple behavior,
but simple behavior is more effective."

＊

Medieval English philosopher and Franciscan monk William of
Ockham (ca. 1285–1349), affectionately known in some scientific
circles as Billy Occam, put forth the idea that the simplest explanation is usually the best explanation. The problem with this idea
is that priests of any profession need complexity to keep the laity
from performing their priestly magic. If you understood the investment process, there would be no need for investment analysts and
advisers, nor would we need mutual funds or any of the other
priests of the "profession."

Finding a great business and buying it at a great price and then
holding it for twenty years is not that hard to learn and profit from
when all the so-called priests of Wall Street are preaching short-
term investment strategies, which, in truth, are completely geared
for making the adviser, and not the advisee, rich.

No. 61

"There seems to be some perverse human characteristic
that likes to make easy things difficult."

✳

Every profession is ultimately a conspiracy against the laity. Only when something is made difficult to understand is there a need for experts, who can charge high fees for having figured it all out. The greater the complexity, the greater the need for an expert to help guide you through the complexity. Wall Street is in the business of selling its expertise in picking stocks for you to invest in, and because of this brokers have a vested interest in presenting the investment game as being so complicated that it is beyond understanding for anyone but the most savvy of pros. Their scheme is simple—they are going to get rich off making you rich, and they keep you coming back because they have convinced you that the investment game is too complicated to figure out. But no one ever asks why, if they are so smart, do they need other people's money to get rich? Maybe they need your money because the game doesn't have anything to do with you making money off investments. Rather they make their money by the commissions they charge you to move you in and out of investments. As Woody Allen once said, "A stockbroker is someone who invests other people's money until it's all gone."

No. 62

"Recommending something to be held for thirty years is a level of self-sacrifice you'll rarely see in a monastery, let alone a brokerage house."

✳

Your stockbroker would starve to death before he would adopt Warren's strategy of buy and hold. It's not that brokers don't believe it will create wealth; it is just that it won't create any wealth for your broker. They make all their money on the commissions they receive by getting you into and out of stocks. The more you get in and out, the more money they make, and they always seem to have a reason to get you into something and out of something else. If your broker has more than one great idea a year, the odds are good he is delusional. If your broker wants to sell you out of a position that he put you into last month because the market conditions have changed, he might be little more than delusional—he might just be dishonest.

Why Not to Diversify

No. 63

"I can't be involved in fifty or seventy-five things.
That's a Noah's ark way of investing—you end up
with a zoo that way. I like to put meaningful
amounts of money in a few things."

✳

If you were to invest in fifty different stocks, then your attention
and ability to keep track of the business economics of each and
every one would be severely limited. You would indeed end up with
a zoo in which none of the animals got the attention it needed. It's
like being a juggler with too many balls in the air. You don't just
drop one—you end up dropping them all.

Warren puts meaningful amounts of money into his investments
because great investment ideas are often few and far between. He
says that you only have to make a few right decisions to end up rich,
and that if you are getting more than one brilliant investment idea
a year, you are probably deluding yourself.

No. 64

"Diversification is a protection against ignorance.
It makes very little sense for those who know
what they're doing."

✳

If you don't understand what you are doing, you should broadly diversify your investments, with the hope that not all your eggs will go bad. If your investment adviser recommends broad diversification, he is really telling you that he doesn't know what he is doing and he wants to protect you from his ignorance. Warren knows what he is doing, so he prefers to concentrate his investments on a few well-chosen eggs, and then he watches them like a hawk.

No. 65

"Wall Street makes its money on activity.
You make your money on inactivity."

✳

The name of the game on Wall Street is to get control of your assets and then milk you for commissions. Brokers have a hundred ways of doing this; they will have you buying and selling on interest-rate news, bad-quarter or good-quarter earnings reports, and every analyst recommendation that comes across their desk. They will even have you trading on the outcome of presidential elections. They make money off activity, any activity, and as long as you are willing to go for it, they are happy to take your money.

For you to make money in the stock market, you need to buy a great company at a fair price or below and hold it for a long time—thereby letting the company's retained earnings build up its underlying value. This is how everyone from Bill Gates to Warren Buffett got superrich. Gates did it with just one stock, and Warren did it on a half dozen. It really does work. Just look at who are the first- and second-richest men in the world. If you still don't believe it, go ask the hundred or so people in Omaha who, thirty years ago, put all their money into just one company, Berkshire Hathaway, and who are now each worth over $50 million.

No. 66

"Why not invest your assets in the companies
you really like? As Mae West said, 'Too much of
a good thing can be wonderful.'"

＊

Warren is famous for highly concentrated stock positions, and he
is willing to keep adding to those positions as long as the economics of the business are there and the price is right. Sometimes he
will build a large position over a number of years, as he did with
Coca-Cola. This is contrary to the strategy of diversifying risk, also
known as not putting all your eggs in one basket. Warren has
always believed that if you diversify just for the sake of diversity,
you will end up with a menagerie for a portfolio, never really
understanding any of the businesses in which your money is
invested. He would rather think long and hard about what basket
he is putting his money into, then once he puts it in, he'll watch
that basket like a hawk.

No. 67

"Wide diversification is only required when
investors do not understand what they are doing."

✳

If some investment advisers are trying to sell you on the idea of
diversifying your stock portfolio, it is because they don't know
what they are doing when it comes to investments and they want
to protect you from their ignorance. And if you don't know what
you are doing, diversification is a wise course in that it will offer
you a modicum of protection against losing everything and the
potential for average growth over the long run. However, it is
never going to make you rich because the strategy is based on the
winners and the losers canceling each other out. It will, however,
never leave you poor.

No. 68

"You only have to do a very few things right in your life
so long as you don't do too many things wrong."

*

The principles of life and investing often parallel each other. To succeed in life you really only have to get a few things right. The only way that you can screw it up is to make a series of bad decisions. That doesn't mean that you can't make mistakes, you just can't make too many big ones.

The same goes for investing. Make a few right investments and you can make a fortune. But every time you make an investment decision, there is a chance that you will get it wrong. Make a few bad ones and you will eventually wipe out the gains from the few good ones you made. Warren decided early in his investing career that it would be impossible for him to make hundreds of right investment decisions, so he decided that he would invest only in the businesses that he was absolutely sure of and then bet heavily on them. He owes 90% of his wealth to just ten of these. Sometimes what you don't do is just as important as what you do.

Discipline, Prudence, and Patience

No. 69

"If you let yourself be undisciplined on the
small things, you will probably be undisciplined
on the large things as well."

✳

Warren has found that people often make exceptions to a disciplined investment strategy when they are making small investments, and that this behavior often leads to an unraveling of a
disciplined approach. Discipline is the key to success in the investment game—just as it is a key to success in much of life. Warren so
believes in a disciplined approach that he has turned down a $2
golf bet because the odds were against him. He freely admits that
on the golf course the odds are usually against him. In Warren's
world little things really do matter.

No. 70

"There is nothing like writing to force you to think
and get your thoughts straight."

✳

If you can't write about it, you haven't really thought about it. This is why every year Warren sits down and writes a long letter to his shareholders explaining the past year's events. This exercise has helped him immensely to fine-tune his thoughts on how to make billions. Writing about something makes you think about it, and thinking about where to invest your money is a good thing, which is why writing about it is even a better thing.

Warren usually begins writing his annual report right after the New Year in his winter home, near the water, in Laguna Beach (right down the street from Benjamin Graham's old place). He writes it in longhand—pen and paper—then ships it out to his friend Carol Loomis, editor at large of *Fortune* magazine. Even a genius needs the helpful hand of an editor.

No. 71

"The less prudence with which others conduct
their affairs, the greater the prudence with which
we should conduct our own affairs."

✳

This is a direct reference to bull stock markets and the insane prices
that they create. In this case, the investing public becomes more
and more imprudent as to what it's willing to pay—meaning that
people are willing to keep buying no matter what the price. In a
bull market, Warren becomes prudent as to what he buys. It stops
him from getting caught up in all the excitement and paying insane
prices that are completely out of line with the long-term economics of the businesses. Prudence in making investment decisions can
save you from folly and make you rich. Imprudence in making
investments decisions can lead to folly and the doorstep of poverty.
And nobody ever got rich by doing things that made him or her
poor.

No. 72

"I've never swung at a ball while it's still
in the pitcher's glove."

✳

Warren has long been a student and fan of baseball, and he took
an important ingredient for his investing strategy from a book that
superhitter Ted Williams wrote, entitled *The Science of Hitting*.
Ted argues that to become a great hitter you have to keep yourself
from swinging at bad pitches—what you are looking for is the perfect pitch. Warren took it as an analogy to investing: To be a great
investor he only had to wait for the right opportunity. He also realized that unlike Ted, who was only allowed three strikes, he could
stand at the plate all day waiting for the perfect investment opportunity to appear.

Thus, Warren never buys into a company if he can't gauge how
the company will perform in the future. He is not a "get in on the
ground floor" kind of guy. He likes a great business with a predictable future that is selling at a discounted price that was brought
on by a correctable mistake by management or an industry recession or a bear market. This is one of the reasons why he stays away
from companies that have no history of making any money. The
ball is still in the glove. He says that if you buy the stock of a company that has never earned a dime, you are essentially buying the
hope that it will make money in the future, that you are buying a
future income stream that might never occur. Future income
streams that might not exist are, and have always been, impossible
to value. If your investment strategy is based on the hope of future
earnings, you are potentially swinging at a whole lot of trouble.

No. 73

"Imagine that you had a car and that was the only car
you'd have for your entire lifetime. Of course, you'd care
for it well, changing the oil more frequently than
necessary, driving carefully, etc. Now, consider that you
only have one mind and one body. Prepare them for life,
care for them. You can enhance your mind over time.
A person's main asset is themselves, so preserve
and enhance yourself."

✳

Warren sees the human mind and body as being a kind of business asset—your business, your assets. You may spend your life selling your services directly to the public, or you may do it indirectly by selling your services to a business that does. But ultimately you are an economic entity that has the capacity for earning huge amounts of money. If you owned a business that had a great potential to make huge amounts of money, you would take great care of it and nurture it and build it into the best business in the world. It is the same thing with your body and mind. They are your business, your assets. You can take care of them and make them strong by seeing that you are well educated, so that you can fully optimize your infinite moneymaking potential, or you can squander your assets and throw away all their potential. The choice is yours.

No. 74

"I buy expensive suits. They just look cheap on me."

✳

Personality always shines through regardless of the quality of the rags. Warren is cheap, has always been, and probably always will be. He is cheap because he knows the future value of a compounding sum of money. In his early days of being a money manager, and in the years after he had made millions, he was famed for driving around Omaha in an old Volkswagen Beetle. Compounding at 20% a year, $25,000 would come to $958,439 after twenty years, and to Warren that is just way too much to pay for a car. As for the expensive suits, he didn't start buying them until he was well past sixty and the future value of the money he spent on them wasn't so great that he couldn't get to sleep at night.

No. 75

"In the search for companies to acquire, we adopt the same attitude one might find appropriate in looking for a spouse: It pays to be active, interested, and open-minded, but it does not pay to be in a hurry."

※

It is one thing to look for something that you will never find, and it is another to look for something that you know from experience you will occasionally see. That is what Warren is looking for—an investment situation that he knows shows up occasionally under the right circumstances. What are the circumstances? A general bear market, an industry recession, a onetime event that doesn't destroy the underlying great business, a panic sell-off—all these things create situations in which the stocks of some really great companies sell for some amazingly low prices. The only thing that he has to do is be patient and wait for those events to occur, which they do—not every day, not every month, and sometimes not every year, but with enough regularity that they have made Warren the second-richest man in the world.

Beware the Folly of Greed

No. 76

"When proper temperament joins up with the proper
intellectual framework, then you get rational behavior."

*

Warren has always said that the best temperament for good investing is to be greedy when others are scared and scared when others
are greedy. That, coupled with an investment philosophy that
focuses on businesses with superior long-term economics working
in their favor, is his secret to successful investing. Buy into great
businesses when everyone else is scared, and stay away from them
when everyone is being greedy. The right temperament will tell you
when and where to pull the trigger—you pull it when people are
scared and are dumping stocks, and you don't pull it when everyone is being greedy and bidding stock prices to the moon.

Twice in Warren's investment career he completely stopped
buying stocks because they had gotten way too high in price. The
first time was at the height of the late-sixties bull market, and the
second time was at the height of the late-nineties bull market. Both
of these timely pullbacks kept him from getting hurt in the crashes
that followed both of those bull markets, and both pullbacks left
him with lots of cash to take advantage of the cheap stock prices
that were right around the corner.

No. 77

"The fact that people are full of greed, fear, or folly is
predictable. The sequence is not predictable."

✳

Warren knows that at times investors are wildly enthusiastic about
a stock and overprice it. He also knows that at times people
become overly fearful and grossly undervalue a stock. What he
doesn't know is when that will happen—just that it will happen—
and when it happens, he is standing there ready to take advantage
of the low prices that fear and folly bring. Avoid the greed and let
fear and folly create the opportunity. That is the way of the intelligent investor.

A great example of this is Warren's purchase of Wells Fargo's
stock during the banking recession of 1990. No one wanted banking stocks because people were afraid that losses from bad real
estate loans would leave the banks insolvent. Warren chose the one
he felt had the best management and was strong enough to weather
the current financial storm. He invested approximately $289 mil-
lion in Wells Fargo, and within eight years it had more than dou-
bled in value.

No. 78

"A stock doesn't know that you own it."

✳

People often humanize inanimate objects, be they stuffed animals, cars, or stocks. When this happens with a stock, emotional thought replaces rational thought. This is a bad thing when it comes to investments. When it is time to sell, you don't want to hesitate because you "love" the stock. Also, when the stock goes down, there is no reason to be mad at it—it doesn't know you own it. It doesn't experience rejection and neither should you.

No. 79

"When you combine ignorance and borrowed money,
the consequences can get interesting."

✳

Ignorance will blind you from folly—the borrowed money will allow you to blindly follow your ignorance till you reach the point of folly. Folly is where you lose the money, which you owe the bank. And banks, like elephants, don't forget. In our time the greatest act of borrowed-money folly was with an investment group no one had ever heard of called Long-Term Capital, which managed to borrow $100 billion to invest in derivatives and, in an act of supreme unforeseen folly, not only wiped out their investors' capital, but also came close to bringing down the country's entire financial system. When working with borrowed money, that which can go wrong often does go wrong. And when it does go wrong, it is never pretty.

No. 80

"Of the seven deadly sins, envy is the silliest, because if you have it, you don't feel better. You feel worse. I've had some good times with gluttony . . . we won't get into lust."

*

Greed is a wonderful thing if it is thy servant and not thy master. You can't get rich without a dose of it, and you can't be happy if you have too much of it. Too much greed leads to envy, and envy is a road paved with the inadequacy of never having enough. The name of the game is to be consumed with passion for making money, rather than being consumed with envy because of what the other guy or gal has in the piggy bank. The happiest rich people are those who love the business life that goes with making money and haven't the least interest in other people's wealth. Besides, what fun is it to be rich if being rich means being miserable with envy?

As for gluttony, Warren's steady diet of Cokes and hamburgers and inch-thick steaks and an endless stream of french fries keeps a smile on his face—he says that he developed a taste for this particular cuisine at a childhood birthday party—but it scares to death Berkshire's health-conscious shareholders who want to profit off their chairman's wisdom as long as possible. Warren—forever rational—says that the increase in life expectancy that a shift to a health-conscious diet might bring is not worth the decrease in the pleasure he would get from eating less junk food. Mark Twain felt the same way about drinking and cigars.

No. 81

"We simply attempt to be fearful when others are greedy
and to be greedy only when others are fearful."

✳

Remember, when prices are in the sky, it's time to say good-bye.
But when prices fall, it's time to give your broker a call. During a
bull market people are being greedy and are driving stock prices
higher and higher, which attracts more and more people to the
game. During these times Warren is fearful and stays away from the
market.

It's during a bear market that other investors are fearful because
no one wants to own any stocks. They sell like crazy, without any
regard for the long-term economic worth of the underlying business. At times like these Warren is in the market being greedy, buying all the fantastic businesses that he has always dreamed of
owning—fearful when others are greedy, and greedy when others
are fearful.

When to Sell,
When to Leave

No. 82

"The most important thing to do if you find
yourself in a hole is to stop digging."

※

If you find you're in a bad investment, the worst thing in the world
to do is continue to throw money at it. Though it's painful to pull
out, in the end it is far more profitable to leave the party and cut
your losses before things go to zero. In the early eighties, Warren
invested heavily in the aluminum industry. It was a mistake, and
when he realized it, he stopped digging and got out. Have the
courage to admit you were wrong—and do it before Dame Fortune
whispers that you have just gone broke.

No. 83

"If at first you do succeed, quit trying."

✳

Warren has always searched for excellent businesses to buy, and then once he bought them, he has held on to them, watching the stock prices grow along with the earnings. Once you make a good investment in an excellent business, it is better to rest on your merits than to sell the business for a modest profit and go looking for another company to invest in. This is why it is important to know what an excellent business is—so you know when you finally get one. But if you find yourself in a mediocre business that doesn't have great long-term economics working in its favor, you had best follow the advice of Bernard Baruch (the Warren Buffett of his day), who, when he was asked how he got so rich, replied with a sly smile, "I always sold too soon."

No. 84

"I buy stocks when the lemmings are
headed the other way."

✳

Warren Buffett knows the time to buy a stock is when everyone
else is selling it—not when everyone else is buying it. All the great
Buffett buys have been on bad news—he likes to buy when things
look darkest—and he can do that because he has studied the world
of business and knows which businesses will survive the adversity
that has brought them to the edge of the abyss and which ones will
go on and take the plunge into corporate oblivion. His big buys
were during the bear markets of 1966, when he bought into Disney; in 1973, when he bought into the Washington Post Company;
in 1981, when he bought into General Foods; in 1987, when he
bought into Coca-Cola; and in 1990, when he bought into Wells
Fargo.

No. 85

"Most people get interested in stocks when everyone else is. The time to get interested is when no one else is. You can't buy what is popular and do well."

✳

The wise investor avoids the popular stocks and the mass hysteria that goes with them, for the popularity that surrounds these stocks often makes them way overpriced! If you want to own a company, look for a period in which the company is no longer popular—that is when you will get the best price and the greatest upside potential. This is why Warren loves a bear market; he has his eye on certain companies that are wonderful businesses that he would buy in a second if he could buy them for the right price. In fact, if you run through Berkshire's portfolio, you will see that all the companies in which he owns shares were bought either during a market crash or a time when the company wasn't a popular investment. His shares in the Washington Post Company, Coca-Cola, Disney, American Express, General Foods, Wells Fargo, Interpublic Group, and GEICO were all bought in either a bear market or at a time in which the company was unpopular with the rest of the investment community.

No. 86

"We don't go into companies with the thought of effecting a lot of changes. That doesn't work any better in investments than it does in marriages."

✳

Warren has found that in most cases the underlying economics of the business remain constant regardless of the manager in charge. A great business will produce great results regardless of who is in charge, and a poor business will produce mediocre results with even the best manager at its helm. Over the last hundred years, Coca-Cola has gone through dozens of managers, some great and some not so great, yet it remains a wonderful business. The Washington Post Company lost its publisher and owner, Katharine Graham, and it remained a fantastic business. However, the auto manufacturers and airlines remain troubled businesses decade after decade in spite of all the brilliant managers who have been in charge. When investing, you choose the great business and you avoid the poor business, even if it is being run by a genius.

No. 87

"Risk comes from not knowing what you are doing."

✳

In the game of buying unpopular stocks, if you don't have the ability to ascertain the long-term economics of the business, you are engaging in some risky business. You won't know whether you paid too much for it until it is too late. Understanding what you are investing in is the only way to remove the risk. As Warren says, "I never buy anything unless I can fill out on a piece of paper my reasons why. I may be wrong, but I would know the answer to 'I'm paying $32 billion today for the Coca-Cola Company because. . . .' If you can't answer that question, you shouldn't buy it. If you can answer that question, and you do it a few times, you'll make a lot of money." Questions compel us to think, but answers tell us whether to act. The trick isn't so much finding the right investment, but knowing when you have found the right answer to the right question.

No. 88

"The only time to buy these is on a day with no *y* in it."

✳

Here Warren is talking about an initial public offering of a company's stock or bonds through an investment bank. He figures that the investment banker doing the selling has already fully priced the issue. There is no chance that an investor is going to get a bargain price. For this reason Warren has stayed away from IPOs since he began his investment career. Warren likes to wait until the securities have traded for a while and the shortsightedness of the stock market has had a chance to misprice the securities downward. The rule is simple: Investment bankers will never serve you a bargain, but the stock market will.

No. 89

"We also believe candor benefits us as managers:
The CEO who misleads others in public may
eventually mislead himself in private."

✳

A CEO who is honest with the public about his mistakes is more likely to learn from them. But if the CEO is always trying to blame someone or something else for his own mistakes, then it is a good sign that he will probably lie to himself about other important things and will most certainly never be honest with the shareholders. This is especially true in all matters of accounting—a willingness to misrepresent one set of numbers will eventually lead to a willingness to misrepresent all the numbers. Or as Warren says, "Managers that always promise to 'make the numbers' will at some point be tempted to make up the numbers." When managers make up the numbers, they go to jail, but sadly enough, their deceptive accounting isn't usually discovered until after they have wiped out their shareholders' investments and their employees' pension funds.

No. 90

"That which is not worth doing at all is not
worth doing well."

❋

Many people spend years working hard for businesses with poor
inherent economics, which means the prospects for making money
are equally poor. So why get good at something that is not going
to benefit you? Why learn to be good at a business that has inher-
ently poor economics and is never going to make you any money?
If you find yourself sailing on a business ship that is going nowhere,
you should jump ship and find one that is headed to the seas of
good fortune—instead of trying to become captain of a slow boat
to a financial nowhere.

This was Warren's experience with Berkshire's textile business.
No matter how good it became, or how many innovations it imple-
mented, or how much capital was thrown at it, the results were
always the same—its competitors could produce textiles cheaper
overseas than they could in America. It became a business that was
not worth doing, and, as Warren said, he painfully had to shut it
down.

No. 91

"A good managerial record is far more a function of what business boat you get into than it is of how effectively you row. Should you find yourself in a chronically leaking boat, energy devoted to changing vessels is likely to be more productive than energy devoted to patching leaks."

※

The best jockey in the world is never going to win races riding a lame horse. But even a mediocre jockey can win races riding a champion. When you get out of school, get a jump on the pack and go to work for a company that has great underlying economics, for no matter what your level of ambition, the great economics of the business will always make you look good and pay you more. If you are already working in a business with great economics, be very careful if you decide to leave the fold. What looks like a better job just might be that chronically leaking boat that Warren warned you about, and no matter how hard you row, you are going to go nowhere.

Mistakes to Beware Of

No. 92

"We never look back. We just figure there is so much
to look forward to that there is no sense thinking of
what we might have done. It just doesn't make any
difference. You can only live life forward."

✳

Warren has never had much use for regrets in life, business, and
investments. In the world of investments there is always some
investment that you missed, some stock going up that you don't
own. If you sold a stock and it then continued going up, you could
spend months kicking yourself. If you didn't sell and the price of
the shares tanked, you could spend years kicking yourself and
everyone else. The same thing applies with business decisions—if
you make a hundred decisions and ten turn out bad, you could end
up obsessing over your mistakes to the point that you neglect the
new decisions that need to be made.

In the investment world, each day brings a new batch of
opportunities in an endless procession. You need not focus on your
mistakes any more than is necessary to learn their lessons. What
you need to do is apply the lessons learned to the problems of
today. In the investment game you will make countless errors of
omission, none of which will hurt you. It is the errors made in taking action that you have to watch out for, and they are found on
the road ahead.

No. 93

"I want to be able to explain my mistakes. This means
I do only the things I completely understand."

✳

If you don't understand what you are doing, then why are you
doing it? The proper investment approach is not intuitive—it is
rational mixed with the right temperament. Ignorance is bliss,
unless you are investing. Then it usually leads to nightmares. If you
want to be able to explain what you did wrong, you need to know
how to explain what you did right, and why you did it in the first
place. You need to know a good business from a bad one, and you
need to be able to determine if a company is underpriced or overpriced. If you can't do that, then you should find someone who
can do it for you, otherwise you are just throwing dice at a craps
table where the odds are always stacked against you.

No. 94

"If you don't make mistakes, you can't make decisions."

✳

Some people can make decisions and some people can't. The ones who can will lead, and the ones who can't will follow. Part of making decisions is making mistakes, for anyone who has to make a dozen decisions in a day will sometimes be wrong. Be wrong too many times, though, and you won't be the leader anymore—your followers will find someone to replace you. A CEO can make mistakes as long as he also makes a lot of money for his shareholders. The important part is making the decision so that you can get on to the next decision. If you procrastinate, then you have decided not to decide. Do this a number of times and things start to stack up. Nothing gets done, the business stops making money. If you make a decision and it turns out to be wrong, Warren says that it is best not to dwell on it, that you should move on to the next one. When Seymour Cray, the brilliant designer of the Cray supercomputer, was asked what separated him from the other engineers, he replied that it was his willingness to embrace mistakes as part of the experimental process. Cray said that the other engineers would stop after the third try, but that he would keep on going until he got it right, even if he made a hundred mistakes. The road that leads to great success is usually paved with a ton of mistakes, so get over it and on with it. If you don't like leading, you can always follow.

Your Circle of Competence

No. 95

"Investment must be rational;
if you don't understand it, don't do it."

※

Warren makes it a point to understand each and every business in which he invests. It's perhaps the greatest key to his success. If he doesn't understand something, he doesn't invest in it. This tenet has famously kept him from investing in high-technology companies—he doesn't understand what they do. He stays away from industries that are changing rapidly and thus are unpredictable. He likes a sure thing—a business that he understands and that is selling at an attractive price. He leaves the dice game to the other guys.

This rationale has saved Warren from venturing into the Internet or other high-tech bubbles. He couldn't rationally buy into a business that might never make any money, nor could he pay forty times earnings for a business that might be made obsolete by the next tech revolution. Let's say that today you can buy the entire company of Yahoo! for $44 billion and it would earn you $1.8 billion a year—do you pull the trigger? You can also invest $44 billion in ten-year U.S. Treasury bonds and make $2.2 billion a year risk-free. Which one looks like the better investment? Which one looks like the gamble? Which one do you understand and which one do you not understand? Which investment is rational and which one isn't? Yahoo! might be part of forgotten tech history in ten years—but the United States should still be going strong. See, it isn't that hard to think like Warren Buffett.

No. 96

"If you understand an idea, you can express it
so others can understand it."

✳

This is Warren's way of testing whether he really understands a business before investing in it. If he can't explain it, he doesn't really understand it. He will not invest in a business he doesn't understand—nor should you. In the struggle to be able to express an idea, you must acquire a fair degree of understanding, which is a good thing if it is an investment idea. This standard requires that you do your research before you buy the stock. Warren's rule is simple: Can't explain it—stay away from it.

No. 97

"If they need my help to manage the enterprise,
we are probably both in trouble."

✳

Just because you are a great investor doesn't mean that you are a skilled business manager. Recognizing talent is different from having talent. A great investor has to be able to recognize talent—the way a football coach has to be able to recognize a great player. Warren knows what to look for in a manager—but he isn't good at running the ball himself. Knowing your abilities and the abilities of others and being able to exploit both to their advantage is the key to running a highly successful business. Warren says his secret for growing a corporation through diverse acquisitions is to buy a good business, for a reasonable price, that already has competent management running it, then get out of the way and let them do their thing. Consider this: When Berkshire subsidiary McLane Company's CEO, Grady Rosier, phoned and asked if it would be okay if he bought a couple of new corporate jets, Warren told him, "That is your decision, it is your business to run."

Though Berkshire has about 180,000 employees, only 17 of these are at headquarters. Warren essentially leaves his managers alone to run their businesses, putting them in charge of all operating decisions. It is easy to manage a giant corporation if you let other people do all the heavy lifting; the trick is having the right managers and then leaving them alone to do their jobs.

No. 98

"Our method is very simple. We just try to buy
businesses with good-to-superb underlying economics
run by honest and able people and buy them at
sensible prices. That's all I'm trying to do."

＊

To know if a business has good-to-superb underlying economics, it
is necessary to understand the business. To know if it is being run
by honest and able people, it is necessary to understand the business. To know if it is selling at a sensible price, it is necessary to
understand the business. Understanding the business is one of the
keys to Warren's success. If he didn't understand the business, he
would not be able to determine if the long-term economics of the
business were good, the management was capable and honest, and
it was selling at a price that was attractive.

The businesses that Warren understands are the ones he pulls
within his circle of competence; all the businesses he doesn't
understand fall outside the circle and should belong to someone
else.

No. 99

"If we can't find things within our circle of competence,
we don't expand the circle. We'll wait."

✳

Warren relies on a circle of competence in making investments. If a company is within his circle, he might buy it if it is selling at the right price; if it isn't within his circle, he won't even look at it. Remember, he is buying into businesses that are not popular at the moment, and he has to know the underlying economics of the business well enough to determine what its future will look like. He can't do this with a business that he doesn't understand. And if he can't find an investment he understands and that is selling at an attractive price, he will wait, and wait, and wait, till one shows up. In 1967 he wrote to his investment partners telling them that he was returning their money since it was getting harder and harder to find investments that he understood and that were selling at attractive prices. He then stood on the sidelines until 1973, when the entire stock market collapsed and suddenly even the best companies were selling at bargain prices. In the investment game it pays to be stubborn and principled and patient in choosing a company to invest in. Pick the wrong company at the right price and you lose; pick the right company at the wrong price and you lose. You have to pick the right company at the right price to win. And to do that you sometimes have to wait and wait and wait . . . along with Warren. Patience, in this game, pays.

No. 100

"Any business craving of the leader, however foolish, will be quickly supported by studies prepared by his troops."

✳

If you make your living pleasing the boss, you will certainly please the boss by supporting his position, regardless of your true feelings. You get nowhere in the business world by being the guy who says "I told you so." You get ahead by being the guy who says "That's a brilliant idea, J.R.!" And if the idea wasn't brilliant, you get to be the guy who says "Don't feel bad, boss, we all thought it was a great idea." Misery loves company, even to the point of stupidity. That is why Warren looks in the mirror when he wants advice— it's speedier, cheaper, and right or wrong, it always leads to the same brilliant decision. And if you can't be your own boss at work, you should at least try to be your own boss in life.

No. 101

"In the business world, the rearview mirror is
always clearer than the windshield."

※

In the business world hindsight is always perfect. But the future is always hidden in a rapidly changing environment. It is hard to tell where you are going if you can't see the road ahead. This is one of the reasons why Warren has always stayed away from technology stocks. He simply has no idea what the road ahead looks like, and neither, he says, does his best friend, Bill Gates, a man who knows a thing or two about technology. This is why Warren stays with the tried-and-true products. He can see where they are going to be in fifteen years. Do you think people are going to stop shaving? Stop drinking Coke? Stop buying car insurance? Stop chewing gum? Stop taking their kids to Dairy Queen on a hot summer night? Highly unlikely. Warren is not interested in products that have a dirty windshield; he is interested in those products that allow him to see the road ahead. With these products he can determine the long-term economic value of the business and whether the short-sighted stock market has mispriced its shares.

No. 102

"I'm very suspect of the person who is very good at one business—it also could be a good athlete or a good entertainer—who starts thinking they should tell the world how to behave on everything. For us to think that just because we made a lot of money, we're going to be better at giving advice on every subject—well, that's just crazy."

*

This goes back to Warren's investment theory of only investing in companies that he understands, that are within his circle of competence. He won't invest outside his circle of competence, and he won't give advice outside his circle of competence. It might just be his secret for always appearing brilliant—just stay with what you know. It also goes to the obnoxious folly of the rich assuming that money makes you intelligent on all things.

Mrs. B. died richer than most of the Harvard-educated kings of Wall Street, and she couldn't read and write. But she did know everything in the world about how to make a profit by buying and selling furniture. In fact, it was cheaper to buy furniture from her in Omaha and have it sent to my home in San Francisco than it was to shop locally. When I asked her how she could make money selling so cheap, she said that the secret was in the buying. If she got it at a low enough price, she could sell it at a lower price than her competitors and still keep her margins. How did she always get the low price? Her competitors bought on credit and paid full price; she paid cash, bought large quantities, and always got a big discount. She also owned her own building so she didn't have to pay rent, which kept her costs even lower. And, yes, she really couldn't read or write, but, boy, she could sure count money.

The lesson here is stick with what you know and you will never look stupid, and you may even end up superrich, even if you can't read or write.

No. 103

"It won't be the economy that will do in investors;
it will be investors themselves."

✳

It will be investors jumping from one stock to another, overpaying
for companies that haven't a hope of ever supporting their stock
market prices with real earnings. It will be the constant drain of
transaction costs that supposed money managers charge their
clients in the name of helping them not get rich. It will be the
unwillingness of investors to do any homework on what they are
investing in, which means that they will blindly buy things based
on popularity and not fundamentals. It will be that taste of instant,
easy money that comes through speculation that will cause them
to gamble more and more sums until they are financially over-
extended. It will be investors panicking that everyone else is leaving the party ahead of them, which will cause them to dump their
stocks at ridiculously low prices. It will be getting caught up emo-
tionally in investing instead of looking at it rationally as buying
fractional interests in businesses. It will be their shortsighted quest
for quick profits blinding them from the long-term economics of
the business. These are the things that will bring them down, not
a change in the GNP or the consumer price index or whether the
Fed has raised interest rates a quarter point.

The Price You Pay

No. 104

"For some reason people take their cues from
price action rather than from values.
Price is what you pay. Value is what you get."

✳

Warren believes that how much you pay determines the amount of
value you get—pay too much and you get little value; the less you
pay, the more value you get. If a business earns $10 million a year
and you buy it for $100 million, the price you paid is $100 million
and the value you got is $10 million a year. If you paid more, say,
$150 million, you would be getting less for your money than if you
paid less, say, $75 million. Pay more, get less. Pay less, get more.
The secret to the game is to always pay less and get more.

No. 105

"That which goes up doesn't necessarily
have to come down."

※

Warren said this in reference to Berkshire Hathaway's stock price.
It has risen from $19 a share in 1965 to $95,000 a share in 2006.
A company with an expanding intrinsic value—such as Berkshire
Hathaway—can find itself with a stock price that keeps rising and
rising and rising. . . .

No. 106

"The key is that the stock market basically just sets prices,
so it exists to serve you, not instruct you."

✳

To Warren, the stock market is just a place where shares of companies are valued on their short-term economic prospects, which creates lots of price gyrations over the short term, which means prices often get out of line with the long-term realities of the business. Sometimes these short-term price swings push share prices well below the long-term economic value of the business—just as they sometimes push them way above the long-term value of the business. As a rule the stock market tends to overvalue stocks. Warren buys stocks when they go below the long-term value of the businesses, then waits for the market's equalizing forces to return the stock prices back upward to being overvalued. If he gets his hands on an exceptional business when prices are cheap, he will continue to hold the business and let the business's retained earnings increase its underlying long-term value, which will eventually increase the price of the company's stock. Over long periods, the economic power of an exceptional business will correct any short-term underpricing mistakes that the stock market makes. But a business is worth what it is worth over the long term, regardless of what the shortsighted stock market says, and you, not the stock market, are in control of what and when you buy.

No. 107

"At the beginning, prices are driven by fundamentals,
and at some point, speculation drives them.
It's that old story: What the wise man does in the
beginning, the fool does in the end."

❋

A wise man buys when the fundamentals are in his favor; that way
he has a margin of safety as to how low prices can go. Time is also
the friend of the fundamentals in that all prices eventually correct
themselves to reflect the fundamental long-term economic value
of the business as measured by what it will earn. When speculation
steps in, fundamentals are thrown out the window and the rising
price motivates more and more buying. A savvy investor knows
that at some point in time the only real demand is the fundamental demand, and when the speculation demand ends—and it always
ends—the price will fall back to reflect the fundamental demand,
which is sometimes a long way down from the speculative highs.
If you are speculating and are still holding positions when prices
start to fall, you only need to look in the mirror to find the fool.

No. 108

"The smartest side to take in a bidding war
is the losing side."

*

A bidding war means that the price is going higher and higher, as both sides battle it out, which means the return on the investment shrinks lower and lower. The higher the price goes, the less of a good deal it becomes, and if the price gets too high, it can become a really bad deal. The problem with being in a bidding war is that competitive emotions can replace rational thought, and a CEO with a large ego can end up paying an insanely large price with their shareholders' money. It's always easier to pay too much for something when you are using other people's money, and no one ever got rich by paying too much for something.

This same principle works in retail as well: If you got the product for a lower price than your competitors, then you can sell it for a lower price to your customers and beat your competitors out of business and still maintain your margins. This is the business model of Berkshire's Nebraska Furniture Mart. They pay cash when they buy merchandise from their wholesalers, and they buy in huge lots, often an entire month's worth of manufacturing, which means they can negotiate a much better deal than their competitors who are buying on credit. This lets NFM charge lower prices for their goods, which attracts more customers, while maintaining their high margins. They charge less and make more because they paid less to begin with. What you sell it for isn't always as important as what you paid for it, especially in retail.

No. 109

"A pin lies in wait for every bubble, and
when the two eventually meet, a new wave of
investors learn some very old lessons."

✳

A speculative frenzy occurs when the general public goes wild for stocks. People see them running up in price and want to jump on and make some easy money. It happens big-time about once every thirty years, usually with the advent of new technology. In the last hundred years it happened with radio, airplanes, autos, computers, biotech, and the Internet. Stock prices reflect the passion in the casino as opposed to the underlying values of the companies. Warren has missed every speculative bull market since he began investing. For him, the prices that were being paid were for future earnings that might never appear, and, in most cases, did not appear. When earnings failed to appear, the hope that was holding up stock prices vanished, gravity took over, and prices fell earthward—often with stunning velocity.

No. 110

"I never attempt to make money on the stock market.
I buy on the assumption that they could close the market
the next day and not reopen it for five years."

✴

Warren is buying on the assumption that he is buying into a business. The stock market sometimes allows him to do this at a cost below what the whole business would sell for to a private buyer. Warren isn't playing the stock market, but rather institutions that are so shortsighted that they are willing to ignore a company's long-term economics in the never-ending search for the quick buck, the glory of being named top mutual fund of the year. If you buy the right company at the right price, the only thing time does is increase the value of the business, which makes you richer and richer and richer as the stock price increases to reflect the underlying value of the business. But get this: If the stock market closed for five years, the underlying value of the business would still increase. The stock market is just a place where you can get a price quote on what it thinks a company is worth over the short term. If you are holding a stock for five years, it is of no consequence what the market thinks the stock is worth in years one through four. The only time that it matters is when you go to sell the stock.

Long-Term Economic
Value Is the Secret to
Exploiting Short-Term
Stock Market Folly

No. 111

"The stock market is a no-called-strike game.
You don't have to swing at everything—you can wait for
your pitch. The problem when you're a money manager
is that your fans keep yelling, 'Swing, you bum!'"

✳

Money managers are basically slaves to the quarterly and yearly figures. If they have a bad quarter, they lose clients, and if they have a bad year, they lose lots of clients. So fund managers become slaves to their clients' wishes for short-term profit, so they have to play the short-term game of swinging at every marginal pitch that comes sliding across the plate. If they don't, their clients will fire them and find someone who will. Fund managers have been hired to place short-term bets on stocks that might move up in the next three to six months, with the long-term economics of a business not being anywhere near as important as its stock's propensity for price fluctuations.

All this focus on the short-term price fluctuations of a stock creates all kinds of pricing mistakes regarding a company's long-term economic value. Warren exploits these pricing mistakes. If the big fund managers weren't obsessed with the quick buck, Warren would never have been able to make all the great buys that he has built his career on. So if you want to make big money in the stock market, stay away from the professional fund managers and learn to use their shortsighted stock-trading gymnastics to take advantage of their long-term pricing mistakes.

No. 112

"What we learn from history is that people
don't learn from history."

✳

People make the same mistakes over and over in the stock market—
they overpay for a business in the hope of making money on the
short-term price movements of the company's shares. This com-
mon mistake drives the entire market and is perpetuated by mutual
fund managers catering to a shortsighted public. Warren has made
his career out of exploiting this inherent shortsightedness and the
pricing mistakes it causes in relation to a company's long-term economic value.

The history lesson that people never seem to learn is that when
companies are priced far in excess of their long-term economic
value, as often occurs during a bull market, any sudden change in
the wind of expectation can cause stock prices to sink violently,
thus wiping out those investors who paid the high bull-market
prices. When prices get high, Warren stays away from the market;
when they fall, Warren gets interested in buying, and if they fall far
enough, and it is the right company, he buys.

No. 113

"Look at stock market fluctuations as your
friend rather than your enemy—profit from
folly rather than participate in it."

✳

The stock market is a beast that ignores the long-term economic
value of an enterprise and only trades on the short-term prospects
of the business. Bad short-term prospects mean that stock prices can
fall dramatically—all the while ignoring the long-term potential of
the enterprise. This creates buying opportunities in companies that
have good long-term economic prospects but are experiencing a few
short-term problems. Stay away from a company when fools rush
in and drive up the price, and buy when fools rush out and drive
down the price.

Some great examples of Warren using stock market fluctuations to buy in are the 1973–74 market crash, in which he bought
$10 million worth of Washington Post stock, which is now worth
over $1.5 billion; the stock market crash of 1987, when he began
buying what would be $1 billion worth of Coca-Cola stock, which
is now worth a hair over $8 billion; and the banking recession,
when he bought $400 million worth of Wells Fargo stock, which
is now worth a touch over $1.9 billion. Stock market fluctuations
have been very, very good to Warren.

No. 114

"Great investment opportunities come around when
excellent companies are surrounded by unusual
circumstances that cause the stock to be misappraised."

✳

Warren learned that great companies occasionally make correctable
mistakes that—over the short term—destroy the price of their stock.
When this happens, the stock becomes misappraised from a long-
term perspective. The key here is being able to determine whether
the error is correctable. That is why it is important to know the economic nature of the business in which you are investing.

Warren's initial investment in GEICO, the auto insurance company, was made as the company was on the verge of insolvency. It
had a great franchise as a low-cost producer, but in a push to get
more business, it let its underwriting discipline slip to the point
that it was writing insurance on anyone and everyone without
increasing its prices to compensate for the risk. The company
started to lose tons of money. Warren knew that if it returned to
the base concept of the business, it not only would survive but
thrive. And thrive it did, turning Warren's $45 million investment
into $2.3 billion over the next fifteen years. Warren saw that
GEICO had made a correctable mistake that once solved would
not damage the long-term economics of a great business. The
shortsighted stock market only saw the mistake.

No. 115

"Uncertainty actually is the friend of
the buyer of long-term values."

✳

Uncertainty in the stock market creates fear, and fear creates panic selling, which forces prices downward regardless of a business's long-term economic prospects. This chain reaction creates a buying opportunity if the long-term economic value of the business is in excess of its selling price. For it is the long-term economics of the business that will eventually pull the stock price back up in line with the realities of the business. Warren's wealth of knowledge about the long-term economics of a business enables him to be certain about which companies will go back up when other investors are through with their bout of uncertainty.

No. 116

"To many on Wall Street, both companies and stocks
are seen only as raw materials for trades."

＊

Professional money managers tend not to see companies and stocks
as businesses, but as bouncing numbers on a screen on which they
can place bets. Warren makes his money off these gamblers when
they oversell a business and drive down a company's share price to
the point that it is cheap relative to the long-term value of the
underlying business. The casino aspect of the stock market has
been in place since its conception; people simply like to gamble, it
makes things exciting. With stocks you can borrow money, lots of
money, to place your bets, which is great if things go your way, but
real bad if they go against you. This explains why there are such
wild price swings—sometimes money managers have to get out
regardless of the price of the shares. As Warren said, "Think about
a burning theater. The only way to leave your seat in a burning
financial market is to find someone to take your seat, which isn't
easy." This, of course, creates all kinds of buying opportunities for
those who know the true long-term value of a business.

No. 117

"No matter how great the talent or effort, some things
just take time: You can't produce a baby in
one month by getting nine women pregnant."

❋

It takes time for business values to build up—it doesn't happen overnight. Just as children take time to grow into adults, businesses take time to grow in value. But if you buy a great business, eventually the values add up to a handsome sum. In the case of Warren's investment in the Capital Cities/ABC Corporation, he paid $17.25 a share in 1986. He didn't overpay and he didn't underpay. He paid what it was worth—but over time the underlying value of the business increased, and along with it the price of the shares, so that in 1995 it was worth $127 a share, which equates to a 24% annual rate of return. The same was true of GEICO, which took fifteen years for the underlying value of the business to increase his initial investment of $45 million into $2.3 billion. That equates to an annual rate of return of 29%. Great businesses, over time, really do grow up to make their shareholders rich; it just takes a little longer than a month.

No. 118

"If past history was all there was to the game,
the richest people would be librarians."

✳

Understanding business history is important to understanding what
can happen, but it won't tell you what will happen and when it
will happen. That takes some foresight on the part of the investor.
Warren has tried to predict the future by staying with businesses
that make products that don't change over time. Predictable product equates to predictable profits. Think beer, candy, car insurance,
soda pop, chewing gum, and razor blades. This way he is able to
predict the long-term economic future of the business and make
value decisions as to what price he is willing to pay. But if the company is constantly having to change its product or line of products
to stay in business, then it is impossible to predict the future for
even a short time ahead. You make the big money knowing what
lies ahead.

No. 119

"Only buy something that you'd be perfectly happy
to hold if the market shut down for ten years."

✳

Every other year, beginning in the sixties and going on into the
nineties, Warren and a band of fellow devotees of Benjamin Graham would gather to discuss the philosophy and talk the talk. One
of the conceptual questions that they used to pose to one another
was "If you had to put all your money into one stock and go away
to a deserted island for ten years, what would it be?" A variant on
that question is "What would you buy today and feel comfortable
with if they closed the stock market for the next ten years?" These
questions cause you to stop thinking in the short term and start
thinking in the long term. When you start thinking long term, you
start thinking quality and the long-term economic nature of the
business. This leads you to ask whether the company's product has
a durable competitive advantage. This means high margins on a
product that doesn't have to change. This means that the plant and
equipment never go obsolete, which means you never have to
retool and you have low research and development costs. Low
costs mean high margins, and higher margins mean more money.
In 1982 the company that Warren said that he would buy and not
mind whether the stock market closed for ten years was Capital
Cities Communications. In 2006 he would probably say the Coca-
Cola Company, provided he could buy it at a price-to-earnings
ratio of below twenty. Warren doesn't mind lying around on a
deserted island as long as he is getting rich.

No. 120

"The investor of today does not profit
from yesterday's growth."

✳

It is the growth of tomorrow that the investor of today will profit
from. If I bought a business today, the profit I would be taking out
of it is all in the future. I don't make any money off the past. The
question is, will the growth be there, and if it is, what am I willing
to pay for it? If the company has a durable competitive advantage,
the growth will be there, but if you pay too much for the stock, you
essentially reduce the amount of money you will make in the future
on the investment—which reduces your annual rate of return.
Would you spend $100 million for a business if it was only going
to make you $1 million a year? Doubtful. But you would jump on
the chance to spend $100 million for a business that earned $20
million a year. Those are the extremes. The tough calls are on the
ones in the middle, but if you want to be like Warren, you even stay
away from the middle and stick with the easy ones.

No. 121

"I'd be a bum on the street with a tin cup
if the markets were efficient."

✳

In the investment world there is a theory that stock markets are efficient, that the quoted stock price represents exactly what the stock is worth on that day given all the information that is known about it. From a short-term perspective the stock market is fairly efficient, but efficiency created by the short-term perspective often creates pricing mistakes from a long-term perspective. This means that from a long-term perspective the stock market is often inefficient. Warren cites his investment in the Washington Post Company when describing market inefficiency. In 1973 the Washington Post Company owned the *Washington Post* newspaper, *Newsweek* magazine, and four network television stations conservatively worth $500 million—yet the stock market was valuing the entire company at only $100 million. Why so cheap? Because from a short-term perspective, Wall Street didn't think the stock would do much over the next year, and it was right, it didn't. But from a long-term perspective it was a screaming buy, and Warren bought $10 million worth of the stock. Thirty years later that $10 million investment is worth $1.5 billion. The thing to remember is that short-term efficiency often creates long-term inefficiency, which you can exploit to make yourself superrich.

No. 122

"As far as I am concerned, the stock market
doesn't exist. It is only there as a reference to see if
anybody is offering to do anything foolish."

✳

Wall Street is always talking about the stock market being up or
down and its ability to predict which way it will turn next. Warren
isn't the least bit concerned with the direction of the market, he is
only concerned with whether the shortsighted stock pickers who
run the large mutual funds have done anything foolish from a long-
term perspective. To find out, he reads the *Wall Street Journal,*
which does an excellent job of keeping track of all kinds of shortsighted foolishness.

No. 123

"We believe that according the name *investors* to
institutions that trade actively is like calling someone who
repeatedly engages in one-night stands a romantic."

＊

The trading madness that goes with the mutual and hedge funds
is almost boundless. They buy stocks on a quarter-point drop
in interest rates and a month later will sell the same stocks at a
quarter-point rise in interest rates. They utilize a strategy called
momentum investing, which requires them to buy a stock when it
is rising quickly in price and sell it if it is rapidly falling in price. If
there is even the slightest drop in earnings, they sell the stock, and
if there is even a modest rise in earnings, they buy it. If there is a
hint of war, they sell, and if there is a hint of peace, they buy. All
of this is done in the name of becoming the most successful fund
of the year, an honor that will bring in millions in new money to
manage from a public that is so shortsighted that even a bad quarter will send it scrambling out of one fund and into another. This
is not investing, it is speculating under the guise of investing.
Investing is buying a piece of a business and watching it grow; speculating is throwing the dice on the short-term direction of the
stock's price. One will make you superrich, the other will make
the fund managers who are throwing the dice superrich.

No. 124

"We do not have, never have had, and never will have an opinion about where the stock market, interest rates, or business activity will be a year from now."

✳

Imagine being able to make billions off the stock market and not having an opinion on the stock market or interest rates. How can Warren do it? He can do it because everyone else is concerned with stock market gyrations and where interest rates are going to be next year, which means that they end up doing silly things like selling a business that has great underlying long-term economics because the Fed might raise interest rates a quarter point. And when these impressionable investors sell great businesses for some silly reason, Warren is there waiting to buy them, and once he gets his hands on them, he isn't letting go. So if you want to become superrich, just ignore all the rant and rave about where the stock market is or is not going, and forget about the Fed and interest rates, and just focus on determining the long-term economic value of the companies that have a durable competitive advantage and then determine where they are selling in relationship to that value. When they are undervalued, buy them, and when they are overvalued, stay away from them. And if you are diligent and stay with the program long enough, you will eventually acquire a portfolio of fantastic companies that will make you superrich over the long run, just as Warren has done.

No. 125

"Of the billionaires I have known, money just brings out the basic traits in them. If they were jerks before they had money, they are simply jerks with a billion dollars."

✳

Money only makes you more of what you already are. If you were kind and generous before you were rich, you will be even more so after you are rich. But if you were cheap and tight before you were rich, you will still be cheap and tight after you get rich. You only have to think of Ebenezer Scrooge to get the point. Scrooge, on the other hand, had to start seeing ghosts before he got it. At the end of the day good people are good people whether they be rich or poor—but what is important is that they are good people, not whether they are rich or poor.

SOURCES

1. http://en.wikiquote.org/wiki/Warren_Buffett; http://www.brainyquote
   .com/quotes/authors/w/warren_buffett.html; *Forbes* 400, October 27,
   1986
2. Berkshire Hathaway 2004 annual meeting
3. Spoken advice/Mary Buffett
4. Spoken advice/Mary Buffett
5. Berkshire Hathaway 1996 annual meeting
6. Spoken advice/Mary Buffett
7. Spoken advice/Mary Buffett
8. Spoken advice/Mary Buffett; *Buffettology* (New York: Scribner, 1997),
   p. 100
9. http://en.wikiquote.org/wiki/Warren_Buffett; http://chatna.com/theme/
   wallstreet.htm
10. *Forbes,* April 21, 1997; *Lincoln Journal Star,* October 8, 2005
11. http://www.brainyquote.com/quotes/authors/w/warren_buffett.html;
    http://hbswk.hbs.edu/archive/3787.html; http://www.omega
    securities.com/newfall2004.htm; widely quoted. Below quote:
    http://www.smh.com.au/news/Business/If-Mr-Buffett-needs-a-character-
    witness-/2005/04/11/1113071912282.html; http://velvelonnational
    affairs.blogspot.com/2005/04/re-truth-and-warren-buffett.html;
    http://www.awlogan.net/examples/buffett.php; *New York Times,* April
    10, 2005
12. http://www.global-investor.com/quote/2710/Warren-Buffett;
    http://www.aussiestockforums.com/forums/showthread.php?t=4024;
    http://www.ridgewoodgrp.com/on%20the%20lighter%20side.htm;
    widely quoted
13. http://www.brainyquote.com/quotes/authors/w/warren_buffett.html;
    http://www.global-investor.com/quote/2710/Warren-Buffett; *New York
    Times Magazine,* April 1, 1990

14. Warren quoting English philosopher Bertrand Russell; http://www.what quote.com/quotes/Warren-Buffett/39804-Chains-of-habit-are-.htm; http://www.cs.iastate.edu/~ddoty/quotes.shtml; http://centennial .jmu.edu/commission/charge.htm; "Warren Buffett Talks Business," PBSTV University of North Carolina, 1995; http://www.global-investor.com/quote/2710/Warren-Buffett; widely quoted
15. http://money.cnn.com/magazines/fortune/fortune_archive/1998/07/ 20/245683/index.htm; interview with reporter for *Fortune* magazine; Warren Buffett speech, Columbia School of Business, October 27, 1993; widely quoted
16. http://beginnersinvest.about.com/cs/warrenbuffett/a/aawarrenquotes.htm; http://www.angelfire.com/co/simplewealth/buffettips.html; Carol J. Loomis, *Fortune,* April 11, 1986, p. 26
17. http://www.edmpinc.com/generalinvesting/shortcourse.htm; Warren Buffett speech, New York Society of Security Analysis, December 6, 1994
18. Press conference with Bill Gates, 2006; http://www.global-investor.com/quote/2710/Warren-Buffett speech, Columbia School of Business, March 13, 1985
19. The University of North Carolina Center for Public Television, 1995; Andy Kilpatrick, *Of Permanent Value* (Birmingham, AL: AKPE, 2004), p. 812; Berkshire Hathaway 2005 annual meeting
20. http://www.global-investor.com/quote/2710/Warren-Buffett; http://www.incademy.com/courses/Bear-market-investing/A-word-on-bears/18/1015/10002; http://www.doh.com/sp_wit2.html; Bill Gates, "What I Learned from Warren Buffett," *Harvard Business Review,* January/February 1996; widely quoted
21. http://www.brainyquote.com/quotes/authors/w/warren_buffett.html; http://www.steadygains.com/essential.cfm—20k
22. http://www.wallstraits.com/main/viewarticle.php?id=88; http://www .global-investor.com/quote/2710/Warren-Buffett; http://www.kenlet .com/nugget/18–24k
23. http://ihome.cuhk.edu.hk/~s027639/Quotes.htm; http://www.lido advisors.com/advisors/pdfs/October%202004.pdf; *Vanity Fair,* October 1995, p. 152
24. http://www.global-investor.com/quote/2710/Warren-Buffett; http://www.brainyquote.com/quotes/authors/w/warren_buffett.html; http://www.merage.uci.edu/NewsAndEvents/InTheNews/InTheNews .aspx?NewsArticleID=46; http://www.buffettsecrets.com/sound-management.htm; widely quoted
25. Berkshire Hathaway 1993 annual meeting; Andy Kilpatrick, *Of Permanent Value,* p. 805
26. http://investorial.com/value-investing/buffetts-tenets-on-selecting-businesses-part-1/; http://www.angelfire.com/co/simplewealth/

buffettips.html; http://www.beginnersinvest.about.com/cs/warrenbuffett/a/aawarrenquotes.htm; widely quoted

27. http://www.brainyquote.com/quotes/authors/w/warren_buffett.html; http://en.wikiquote.org/wiki/Warren_Buffett; http://investreview.wordpress.com/warren-buffett-quotes/; widely quoted
28. Q&A session with Dartmouth MBA students
29. http://www.dontquoteme.com/search/quote_display.jsp?quoteID=1277&gameID=1; http://www.veritascorp.com/our_philosophy/index.html; widely quoted
30. Berkshire Hathaway 1994 annual meeting; Andy Kilpatrick, *Of Permanent Value*, p. 810
31. http://www.turtlemeat.com/invest/how-to-invest-quotes/87; http://www.global-investor.com/quote/2710/Warren-Buffett; http://money.uk.msn.com/Investing/Insight/Special_Features/Active_Investor/article.aspx?cp-documentid=143189; widely quoted
32. Berkshire Hathaway 2003 annual meeting
33. http:/.../Products/IndustryResearch/IntelligentInvestor.asp?Page=BASICS&Issue=25838; http://www.brainyquote.com/quotes/authors/w/warren_buffett.html
34. Berkshire Hathaway 1995 annual meeting
35. http://www.investingvalue.com/news/2006/08/warren-buffett-quotes.html; http://www.global-investor.com/quote/2710/Warren-Buffett; http://news.com.com/2100–1023–212942.html?legacy=cnet
36. http://about.countrywide.com/InTheNews/Docs/March%202005.pd; http://www.the-tree.org.uk/Sacred%20Grove/treequotes1.htm; http://isaac.org.au/info/quotes.htm; *Vanity Fair,* October 1996; NewsInc., January 1991
37. http://compgeom.cs.uiuc.edu/~bunde/quotes.html; http://www.global-investor.com/quote/2710/Warren-Buffett
38. Berkshire Hathaway 1993 annual meeting; http://www.investorguide.com/daily-archives.cgi?date=032604; http://www.global-investor.com/quote/2710/Warren-Buffet; http://www.armchaireconomist.com/update.htm
39. http://www.businessweek.com/1999/99_27/b3636006.htm; http://www.deanlebaron.com/book/ultimate/chapters/val_inv.html; *Forbes* 400, October 18, 1993, p. 40
40. Berkshire Hathaway 1988 annual meeting
41. *Forbes,* August 6, 1979, p. 25; http://en.wikiquote.org/wiki/Warren_Buffett
42. Warren Buffett speech, New York Society of Security Analysts, December 6, 1994; http://www.leithner.com.au/circulars/circular105.htm
43. *U.S. News and World Report,* June 20, 1994, p. 58; Andy Kilpatrick, *Of Permanent Value,* p. 810
44. http://en.thinkexist.com/quotation/the_smarter_the_journalists_are_the_

better_off/227538.html; http://www.brainyquote.com/quotes/authors/w/
warren_buffett.html

45. Q&A session with Dartmouth MBA students
46. Berkshire Hathaway 1987 annual meeting; Andy Kilpatrick, *Of Permanent Value*, p. 781
47. *Omaha World-Herald*, January 2, 1994, p. 17S; Q&A session with University of Florida students, 1998
48. http://www.afterquotes.com/great/quotes/business.htm; http://en.wiki quote.org/wiki/Warren_Buffett; Carol J. Loomis, "The Inside Story of Warren Buffett," *Fortune*, April 11, 1988, p. 26
49. Berkshire Hathaway 1993 annual meeting
50. Warren quoting Goethe, *Newsweek*, April 1, 1985, p. 56
51. http://www.global-investor.com/quote/2710/Warren-Buffett; *Fortune*, April 11, 1988, p. 26
52. Berkshire Hathaway 2003 annual meeting
53. http://www.greatbusinessquotes.com/work_ethic_quotes.html; http://www.quotationsbook.com/quotes/30589/view; *Forbes*, October 22, 1990; Andy Kilpatrick, *Of Permanent Value*, p. 783; http://www.brainyquote.com/quotes/authors/w/warren_buffett.html
54. Q&A session with Dartmouth MBA students
55. http://money.cnn.com/magazines/fortune/fortune_archive/1998/07/20/ 245683/index.htm; Q&A sessions with Dartmouth and Florida MBA students
56. Q&A session with Dartmouth MBA students
57. http://www.global-investor.com/quote/2710/Warren-Buffett; Berkshire Hathaway 1994 annual meeting
58. *Fortune*, May 5, 1977, p. 250; http://www.nareit.com/portfoliomag/menu/ in_closingmenu.shtml; http://www.expectationsinvesting.com/ chapter5.shtm
59. http://www.brainyquote.com/quotes/authors/w/warren_buffett.html; http://www.prakashgaba.com; http://www.webjunction.org/do/Display Content?id=13852; http://en.wikiquote.org/wiki/Warren_Buffett; widely quoted
60. http://www.cybernation.com/quotationcenter/quoteshow.php?type= author&id=1356; *Channels*, November 1986; http://socialize.morning star.com/NewSocialize/asp/FullConv.asp?forumId=F100000015&last ConvSeq=51946; http://www.brainyquote.com/quotes/authors/w/ warren_buffett.html
61. http://www.brainyquote.com/quotes/authors/w/warren_buffett.html; http://en.wikiquote.org/wiki/Warren_Buffett—38. Woody Allen quote: http://www.llywelyn.net/docs/quotes/woody.html; http://uk.biz .yahoo.com/glossary_mot9.html
62. http://www.brainyquote.com/quotes/authors/w/warren_buffett.htm;

http://marcustoday.com.au/pdf/FamousFinancialquotes.pdf?PHPSESSI
D=450152cd7ebabc613f6fbd05587572cf
63. http://www.leithner.com.au/newsletter/issue53.htm; *Wall Street Journal,*
September 30, 1987, p. 17
64. Berkshire Hathaway 1996 annual meeting; http://www.global-investor
.com/quote/2710/Warren-Buffett
65. Q&A session with University of Florida MBA students
66. http://www.brainyquote.com/quotes/authors/w/warren_buffett.html;
http://beginnersinvest.about.com/cs/warrenbuffett/a/aawarrenquotes.htm
—32k
67. http://beginnersinvest.about.com/cs/warrenbuffett/a/aawarrenquotes.htm;
http://www.brainyquote.com/quotes/authors/w/warren_buffett.html
68. http://www.brainyquote.com/quotes/authors/w/warren_buffett.html;
http://www.whartondc.com/article.html?aid=754—21k
69. *Chicago Tribune,* December 8, 1985, p. 1
70. http://www.leithner.com.au/newsletter/issue44.htm; "Warren Buffett
Talks Business," University of North Carolina, Center for Public
Television, Chapel Hill, 1995
71. Anthony Sampson, *The Midas Touch* (New York: Dutton, 1990), p. 79;
http://www.sigfin.com/newsletters/summer_2002.pd; http://www.jolley
asset.com/id52.htm
72. *Fortune,* March 4, 1996
73. Berkshire Hathaway 2002 annual meeting
74. http://www.brainyquote.com/quotes/authors/w/warren_buffett.html;
Berkshire Hathaway 1994 annual meeting
75. http://www.global-investor.com/quote/2710/Warren-Buffett;
http://www.kenlet.com/nugget/18; http://www.investorguide.com/daily-
archives.cgi?date=122005—32k
76. *Forbes* 400, October 18, 1993, p. 40; www.closebrothers.com.ky/
pubs/Close%20Cayman%20Brief%202003.pd
77. http://en.wikiquote.org/wiki/Warren_Buffett; "The Convictions of a
Long-Distance Investor," *Channels,* November 1986, p. 22
78. Berkshire Hathaway 1995 annual meeting; Andy Kilpatrick, *Of
Permanent Value,* p. 813; http://in.groups.yahoo.com/group/lawarren
buffet/messages/1601?viscount=10
79. http://www.global-investor.com/quote/2710/Warren-Buffett; Berkshire
Hathaway 1995 annual meeting
80. Berkshire Hathaway 2006 annual meeting
81. http://www.brainyquote.com/quotes/authors/w/warren_buffett.html;
http://www.forbes.com/lists/2005/54/C0R3.html—34k
82. http://www.expectationsinvesting.com/pdf/pitfalls.pd; http://www.fool
.com/news/take/2003/take030910.htm*; http://whereiszemoola
.blogspot.com

83. *Forbes* 400, October 19, 2002, p. 93
84. "Buffett Faces Shareholders," *Omaha World-Herald*, May 21, 1986, p. 27; Berkshire Hathaway 1986 annual meeting
85. http://www.global-investor.com/quote/2710/Warren-Buffett; "Omaha's Plains Dealer," *Newsweek*, April 1, 1985, p. 56
86. *Fortune*, April 1988
87. http://www.quotationsbook.com/quotes/34665/view; "Buffett Talks Strategy with Students," *Omaha World-Herald*, January 2, 1994, p. 17S; http://www.brainyquote.com/quotes/authors/w/warren_buffett.html. Lower quote: http://www.tilsonfunds.com/BuffettNotreDame.pdf
88. http://www.quotationspage.com/quote/1274.html—9k; http://www.brainyquote.com/quotes/authors/w/warren_buffett.html
89. http://velvelonnationalaffairs.blogspot.com/2005/04/re-truth-and-warren-buffett.html; http://www.refresher.com/!buffett2.html. Lower quote: http://www.investopedia.com/ask/answers/191.asp; http://www.thephoenixprinciple.com/quotes/
90. http://www.zaadz.com/quotes/Warren_Buffett; http://www.ndir.com/SI/email/q205.shtml; Berkshire Hathaway 2005 annual meeting
91. http://www.bizjournals.com/triad/stories/2003/02/17/story1.html; http://www.global-investor.com/quote/2710/Warren-Buffett
92. Q&A session with University of Florida MBA students
93. http://www.selfgrowth.com/articles/Dunn163.html; www.givernycapital.com/Archives%20des%20citations.ht; *Omaha World-Herald*, December 5, 1968
94. http://online.wsj.com/public/article/SB113175788303495486-_CkAF_S8b1i9OWkJAqsW_qfhox8_20061112.html?mod=blogs
95. http://finance.yahoo.com/columnist/article/richricher/4027; http://www.centman.com/Library/Articles/Aug99/ExtraordinaryValues2.html
96. http://www.leithner.com.au/newsletter/issue44.htm; "Warren Buffett Talks Business," University of North Carolina Center for Public Television, Chapel Hill, 1995
97. Berkshire Hathaway 1991 annual meeting; Andy Kilpatrick, *Of Permanent Value*, p. 803. Below quote: http://online.wsj.com/public/article/SB113175788303495486-_CkAF_S8b1i9OWkJAqsW_qfhox8_20061112.html?mod=blogs
98. December 6, 1994, special meeting of the New York Society of Financial Analysts; http://www.burgundyasset.com/us/aug-95.asp
99. Berkshire Hathaway 1995 annual meeting
100. http://en.wikiquote.org/wiki/Warren_Buffett—38k; http://www.bankdirector.com/issues/articles.pl?article_id=1173; *Los Angeles Times Magazine*, April 17, 1991, p. 36
101. http://quipsmart.com/index.php/archives/2005/05/02/warren-buffett-quotations/—12k; http://www.quotationspage.com/quotes/Warren_Buffett/

102. Q&A session with University of Washington students; http://money
.cnn.com/magazines/fortune/fortune_archive/1998/07/20/245683/
index.htm
103. Berkshire Hathaway 2004 annual meeting
104. http://www.brainyquote.com/quotes/authors/w/warren_buffett.html;
http://www.global-investor.com/quote/2710/Warren-Buffett;
http://home.comcast.net/~standja/quotes/invest_wisdom.htm
105. Said to Mary Buffett regarding price of Berkshire Hathaway stock
106. Berkshire Hathaway 2006 annual meeting; http://www.statesman.com/
money/content/shared/money/stories/hank/hank0714.html
107. Berkshire Hathaway 2006 annual meeting
108. Q&A session with Columbia Business students, October 27, 1993;
http://groups.msn.com/zenwayus/general.msnw?action=get_message&
mview=0&ID_Message=70&LastModified=46; Andy Kilpatrick, *Of
Permanent Value*, p. 807
109. http://www.gemini.co.il/event2005/winning.pdf; http://www.kenlet.
com/share?sort_by=price&menu_string=recent&hide_closed=true&
tags_string=programming—42
110. http://www.brainyquote.com/quotes/authors/w/warren_buffett.html;
http://www.global-investor.com/quote/2710/Warren-Buffett—46k
111. Berkshire Hathaway 1999 annual meeting; http://en.wikiquote.org/
wiki/Warren_Buffett
112. Berkshire Hathaway 2004 annual meeting
113. Warren Buffett speech, New York Society of Security Analysts,
December 6, 1994; http://www.brainyquote.com/quotes/authors/
w/warren_buffett.html
114. "Meeting Charlie Munger," *Forbes,* January 22, 1996, p. 78;
http://www.brainyquote.com/quotes/authors/w/warren_buffett.html
115. http://smartcapitalist.com/blog_18.shtml; http://www.fool.com/
community/pod/2001/010226.htm; *Forbes,* August 6, 1979, p. 25
116. Michael Lewis, "The Temptation of St. Warren," *The New Republic,*
February 17, 1992, p. 22. Below quote: http://www.smh.com.au/
news/Business/Lots-of-laughs-but-no-funny-business/2005/05/01/
1114886252329.html; Berkshire Hathaway 2005 annual meeting
117. http://www.contango.com/investor/events/20050208/ogis020805.ppt;
http://www.capitalideasonline.com/articles/index.php?id=1186;
http://sanjbak.com/Quotes.HTM; http://forum.richdad.com/forums/
tm.asp?m=386495&appid=&p=&mpage=1&key=&
118. http://nvestopedia.com/university/greatest/warrenbuffett.asp;
http://www.brainyquote.com/quotes/authors/w/warren_buffett.html
119. http://www.brainyquote.com/quotes/authors/w/warren_buffett.html;
http://www.woopidoo.com/biography/warren_buffett.htm
120. http://www.quotationsbook.com/quotes/29322/view;
http://www.brainyquote.com/quotes/authors/w/warren_buffett.html

121. http://www.global-investor.com/quote/2710/Warren-Buffett; http://en.wikiquote.org/wiki/Warren_Buffett—38

122. http://www.global-investor.com/quote/2710/Warren-Buffett; http://www.economywatch.com/business-leaders/warren-buffett.html—7k

123. http://www.betterinvesting.org/mutualfunds/blog/archives/2006/05/one_night_stand.html; http://www.global-investor.com/quote/2710/Warren-Buffett; http://www.kenlet.com/nugget/18

124. *Forbes,* October 13, 1997; Andy Kilpatrick, *Of Permanent Value,* p. 781

125. http://www.brainyquote.com/quotes/authors/w/warren_buffett.html; *Forbes,* April 21, 1997; Andy Kilpatrick, *Of Permanent Value,* p. 818

ACKNOWLEDGMENTS

We wish to thank first and foremost Warren Buffett. Although he did not participate in the writing of this book, we are forever indebted to him for his wisdom and generosity. His genius as an investor is overshadowed only by his philanthropy, which will provide future generations with the benefits of his investing passion.

We would also like to thank our publisher and editor, Roz Lippel at Scribner. She is the best in the business and always a joy to work with.

We owe special debts of gratitude as well to: our past publisher, Eleanor Rawson, who helped us conceive the Buffettology series of investment books and who taught us the craft of bookmaking; the amazing Cindy Connolly Cates, who edited our earlier drafts; Richard Fischer for being a saint; and Fritz Perlberg for knowing what a true friend is.

Many people have further educated us in the world of investments and business. Among the notables are: money manager and author Timothy P. Vick, one of the great minds of a new generation; the late Rose Blumkin, founder of the Nebraska Furniture Mart, who gave us a lesson in how to "make a business" in furniture and carpet (no better teacher ever lectured at Harvard); Barnett C. Helzberg, Jr., the former CEO of Helzberg Diamonds, for writing *What I Learned Before I Sold to Warren Buffett,* one of the all-time great books on retailing and a must-read for any serious student of business; and author and historian Andrew Kilpatrick, whose books are mandatory reading for any Buffettologist.

We also owe a tremendous debt to the past deans of the investment world: Bernard Baruch, Philip Fisher, Walter Schloss, and Benjamin Graham. These are the giants upon whose shoulders we stand.

Most important, we wish to thank the gallant Sam Haygood and the enchanting Kate Clark, both of whom make life wonderful.

INDEX

basic math skills needed in, 51
bidding wars in, 139
capital, 30, 34–35, 39
compounding of, 3, 4, 92
conviction in, 23
discipline in, 87
diversification as bad idea in, 79–84
eliminating risk in, 38, 110
in established and consistent businesses, 7, 15, 22, 31, 34–36, 39, 47, 90, 109, 123, 129, 152, 153, 154, 158
greed and fear in, 97–98, 101–2, 131, 149
ideal circumstances for, 93, 146, 147, 149, 150, 158
independent thinking in, 20, 52, 73, 128
inside information on, 44
learning from experience and mistakes in, 54, 57, 65, 117, 119
long-term, 10, 15, 18, 31, 34, 35, 45, 47, 74, 76, 81, 82, 97
mentors in, 43, 45, 46, 47, 48
in offshore companies, 21
outdated principles and, 16, 47
patience in, 4, 10, 15, 18, 90, 93, 127, 145, 151
prudence in, 89
pulling out of, 105, 113
researching and understanding of, 10, 118, 123–24, 126–27, 130, 131, 148
risk in, 38, 110
simplicity in, 74–75
value in relation to price in, 38, 45, 48, 135, 141, 154, 158
vs. speculations, 157
writing about own, 88
see also business; stocks

journalists, 53
junk bonds, 20

lawsuits, 9
Long-Term Capital, 100
Loomis, Carol, 88

McLane Company, 125
managers, 16, 59, 98, 109
good businesses vs. good, 28, 109, 114
hiring of, 58
positive workplace for, 63–66, 125
as proactive, 62
recognizing talent in, 125
weak or creative accounting by, 33, 112
math skills, 51
Maxwell, Robert, 6
mentors, investment, 43, 45, 46, 47, 48
mistakes, 117–19
accepting of, 117, 119
learning from, 54, 57, 65, 117
momentum investing, 157
money, 159
charitable contributions with, 24
compounding of, 3, 4
drawbacks of too much, 24
envy and, 101
happiness and, 12, 101
losing of, 3
marrying for, 17
working with borrowed, 100, 150
see also investments
Munger, Charlie, 57, 71
mutual funds, 74, 157

Nebraska Furniture Mart, 8, 57, 59, 139
negotiations, 5, 6
contracts and, 8
noncompete clauses, 8

offshore companies, 21
Ogilvy & Mather, 15

Pascal, Blaise, 37
patience, in investments, 4, 10, 15, 18, 90, 93, 127, 146, 151
PetroChina, 21
prices:
bidding wars and, 139
value in relation to, 38, 45, 48, 135, 141, 154, 158
see also stock market; stocks
price-to-earnings ratio, 153
proactive management, 62

ABOUT THE AUTHORS

Mary Buffett and David Clark have written three best-selling books on Warren Buffett's investment methods: *Buffettology, The Buffettology Workbook,* and *The New Buffettology.* These books have been published worldwide in ten languages, including Chinese and Russian.

ABOUT THIS BOOK

To Buffettologists, Warren Buffett's aphorisms are more than simple statements of truth; they are akin to the teachings of a Chinese Taoist master, because the more you ponder them, the more they reveal the "path" or "way" to achieving great wealth. This collection of Buffett quotations and interpretations has specifically been selected to help you discover the "way" by taking you deep into the enlightened thinking of the greatest investor and philanthropist of our time. It is the authors' hope that the wisdom contained herein will help enrich your life by making your world a far more profitable, and a more enjoyable, place to live and work.